Out of Darkness, Into the Light

With Letters from Michele

Michele Frantz

Copyright © 2022 by **Michele Frantz**

All rights reserved. No part of this publication may be reproduced, distributed or transmitted in any form or by any means, without prior written permission.

Publisher's Note: This work is a true story as the author recalls it. Many of the names, and places have been fictionalized.

Book Layout © 2017 BookDesignTemplates.com
Book Editing and Formatting by JeanneFelfe.com

Out of Darkness, Into the Light/ Michele Frantz. -- 1st ed.

ISBN 9798788010588 (paperback)

Dedication

I'd like to dedicate this book to my daughter, Darchele. She has put up with me for many years. Bless her, I don't know what I would have done without her.

It is also for those who read my blogs and listen to my podcasts and have asked when my book will be published. This is for them and anyone who has suffered from abuse, to let them know they are not alone, and I hope and pray it will help them find the light.

Contents

Prologue 1

The Beginning of the end of Dad 3

My Family 9

My Grandmother 15

Everyday Life 23

High School 31

Dad's Gone 39

Don the Liar 47

Jack the Alcoholic 59

My Friend Susie 71

Darrow the Schizophrenic 81

Divorced Darrow 91

Home Again 105

Paula the Sneak 115

In the Darkness 125

Finding the Light 149

Home Again with Mom and Bill 163

Cooper's 169

A. R. Mason, Inc. 193

In the Light 219

Acknowledgements 229

About the Author 231

Prologue

One evening as I sat in my study reading, it suddenly occurred to me that I was happy; maybe it was contentment. I do not mean just for the moment, but the kind of feeling that is a part of your very being. I don't recall ever feeling this way before. It seems that it's harder and harder to remember the unhappiness and the years of paralyzing fear that prevented me from having a fulfilling life.

My full name is Caroline Michele (Humbert) Frantz. I have gone by seven different names. From birth to the seventh grade I went by my first name, Caroline. My family still calls me that. In the eighth grade I started going by Kay—I thought that made me a different person, but it was a fruitless attempt to change my life. After I graduated and started working, I went by Carol or Carolyn.

At nineteen, when I went to New Mexico, I started using my middle name, Michele. When I moved to California, and got married the first time, some of my friends started calling me Mitch, which I liked. When I divorced and moved back to Michigan and got married again, my in-laws called me Mike, but everyone else called me Michele. It has been Michele for the better part of the last fifty-five years.

By the time I graduated high school, we had moved ten times, and I'd gone to seven different schools. As an adult, I've moved thirty-eight times and had twenty-two jobs. I also dated twenty-one men who I saw enough to remember and had some one-night stands.

The letters in my book are relative to the time they were taking place. Early letters are the pleadings of my unhappy inner child, Caroline, desperately seeking love. No matter how hard I tried, I failed. With all the moving we did, I never felt I had a place where I belonged. Until I was in my forties, all my attempts to find the love I so desperately longed for failed.

Although my story is not unique, it is mine and told in my unique way. Thousands of children have been abused in many ways, but my story is not so much about the abuse, it is more about the effects and the recovery.

I hope that you will gain some insight into your own life while reading my story and that it will help you seek the help that will lead you out of the darkness and into the light.

The Beginning of the end of Dad

April 1960

Daddy, can't you hear my cries,
Oh my God, this was the worst beating yet. How could you do this to me? Can't you see that I need your love? What's wrong with me? Please, I can't take it anymore. I hate you, and I hate myself for being so stupid and ugly. I bet if I was smart and pretty you would like me.
I'm not going to hide what you did to me this time, and you're not going to get away with it.
Kay

I was older and braver now and said "no" to my dad once. He slammed me up against the wall and said, "If you ever say no to me again, I'll break every bone in your body." I believed him, and that was the end of my brave spell.

When I was a senior, I had a birthday party for my best friend that turned out awful—not the party but what happened afterward. There were six of us, and since we were young adults (so I thought), I asked my mother if we could have the party in the living room, instead of the basement. She agreed. That evening we had quite a good time pretending to be all grown up. My mother was in the basement during the party, so if she thought something was wrong, all she had to do was walk upstairs. One of the young men had his mother purchase Kady a gift; it was a cute pair of baby doll pajamas. Kady ran into my bedroom and slipped the top over her clothes to see if it fit. He said, "If it doesn't fit my mom will exchange them." We all had a good laugh. They fit and were really cute.

After everyone left and everything was back in order, I went to bed. I lay down and pulled the covers up. "Ohhh," I sighed as I snuggled in. It was a nice party. Bedtime was my favorite time of the day. It was safe, and I could go anywhere I wanted when I slept. I learned when I was very young how to make myself dream whatever I wanted to dream. It was like a secret life. I loved to tell stories, and all I had to do was start the story when I was awake, and as I drifted off to sleep, my dream would take off.

About three a.m., a hand latched onto my arm and jerked me off the bed. I scrambled to get my footing. My father was angry. He had a board in his hand and started swinging. I put my free arm up to block the board, and it came down across my upper arm. I stumbled, and another struck me on the hip, followed by many more blows. I had bruises on my arms, chest, back, and upper legs. One time he missed me and knocked a hole in the closet door.

He was usually careful not to leave marks where others could see them, but he was out of control this time. I caught a look at his face, and it was awful, so full of anger and hate; it was as if someone had drawn a line across his face, and one part was red and the other white. His dark eyes were vacant, and his brows furrowed. When he was finished, he left me there on the floor and walked out. He never said a word the whole time.

I bit my lip and tried not to cry until he was gone. I got up and looked at myself in the dresser mirror, and through my tears could see marks on my arms and sides already showing. I hurt everywhere. *I'm not even safe in my bed anymore. He is not going to get away with it this time.*

In the morning, while everyone got ready for school and work, he looked at me and said, "Wear a long sleeve blouse to school today."

I thought, *what's wrong, are you ashamed of what you did?* I wore a sleeveless blouse to school that day and later wished I hadn't. My arms were a mass of bruises.

Every time someone would say, "My God, what happened?" I would start crying. I found myself in the nurse's office and from there to the principal's office.

"What happened?" the principal asked.

I told him the truth. "My dad beat me with a board."

At first, he did not believe me because he was a friend of my father's.

"If you don't believe me, go ask my father what happened."

My father was the superintendent of that school district, and his office was located in the high school. I don't know what happened when the principal confronted my father, but within two months, my father was superintendent in another school district in a nearby town. His secret was out, at least in my school.

My mother spent the next day in her room crying and never mentioned she knew what had happened.

I was terrified because his friend knew my father was a monster now, and every minute I remained in that house could be my last.

After a week of living in pure terror, I ran away to a friend's house. My father guessed where I was and would drive by and make threats when he saw my friend's dad in the yard. My friend's dad said I wasn't there. My dad said he would get a restraining order so they could not get anywhere near me.

Her parents finally said I couldn't stay or they might get into trouble.

I waited until my father was in front of their house and then ran out the back and over the fence to the next street where my friend's boyfriend was waiting. He drove me to her grandmother's house.

Her grandmother talked to me for a long time about my options, which were few. She said, "If you're afraid to go home, go to the police."

Though the whole idea of going to the police was scary, I took her advice. I told the police officer, "I don't know where to go, and I'm afraid to go home."

The officers could see evidence of the bruises on my arms, and one officer asked, "Do you want to press charges?"

"No," I responded, as I was afraid to press charges.

They said they would talk to him. The officer called my father and he came down to the police station. I could hear them shouting at him from another room. When they brought him in to face me, the officer said, "Next time she shows up in school looking like this, she won't need to press charges. I will find you and arrest you."

On the way home, I couldn't look at him, and no one spoke. I was terrified, and my heart pounded as I sat glued to the door. *If he so much as looks at me wrong I'm out the door, car moving or not.*

That was the last time he ever hit me. He even lightened up on the verbal abuse. I think he was trying to act as if I did not exist. I believe he knew it was over and made his decision to leave us. It was just a matter of when. I wish he had left right then.

My Family

January 1947

Hello, is anyone out there?

I don't know what I did or why Daddy doesn't like me anymore? What is wrong with me? What did I do that was so wrong? Why doesn't anyone love me? I feel so lonely and unwanted. I don't know what to do. How can I make this better? Mommy, I need you, please help me. I promise I'll be good, just love me. Please, won't someone help me?

Daddy hates me, and Mommy doesn't love me.
I want to be held and loved. Please!
Caroline

My father was superintendent of the public schools, and we attended church regularly. We appeared to be the picture-perfect family. If people could only see behind closed doors. Underneath a pleasant persona, he was cold, calculating, and used people to further his own needs, with a complete disregard for their feelings. His many affairs left women heartbroken. He demanded perfection from his family, and when he did not get it, he became violent, mean, and vindictive.

He came from a highly educated family and was brought up by his mother and two sisters, ten and fifteen years older. He never had a hand raised to him, and they all thought he was wonderful.

He was a handsome egotistical abuser, who profoundly affected my life. He thought he could do no wrong. He earned a Ph.D., and everyone called him doctor, which just fed into his already oversized ego. The community respected him.

When I was in high school, I referred to my father as Dr. Jekyll and Mr. Hyde. Dr. Jekyll—the one he showed to the public—had a pleasant face, and smiled a lot. Mr. Hyde—the one he let out at home—had a stern face, with cold and unfeeling eyes, who rarely smiled, and when he did, it did not look natural.

Mother was pleasant looking with what she called dirty blonde hair. Raised on a farm, she was the first in her family to graduate from high school.

I remember that she cared for the home, cleaned, cooked, washed, and ironed—a typical homemaker. I recall very few interactions with her, and the ones I remember were not always nice. I don't remember ever being comforted or hugged by her.

One day I did something that made my mother mad. She tried to hit me, and when I dodged her swing, I fell to the floor. She kicked me and said, "I don't have to love you because you are my daughter. You have to earn that love." I will never forget that. I had just learned that there is no such thing as unconditional love. That was the only time I ever remember her striking me. Now my father—that was a different story.

In my mother's defense, back in those days, there were no shelters to protect women with children from their abusers. She could not go back home to her parents with three little kids. I am sure she felt trapped.

The three of us kids reacted to the abuse very differently. My younger brother, Herb, was quite popular in school. He was obnoxious, loud, and annoying, but he was my brother, and I would stand up for him any day. You know that old saying "blood is thicker than water." Unfortunately, he had some of my father's tendencies. From what I understand, when he got married, his wife set him straight the first time he hit one of his boys, and he never did it again.

He does not remember our childhood the same as Ken, my older brother, and I do. He didn't think it was terrible. Well, Ken and I saved him from a lot of abuse by taking the blame.

Herb was the only one who could get to me. He would do things to make me mad because he knew he could, and I would end up throwing things at him. Once I threw a clock at him and just as it reached him, he shut his bedroom door. BLAM! Of course, the clock shattered all over the door. Once I threw a quart of milk down the basement stairs at him. Yuk, was that a mess, and I had to clean it up. Once I swung one of my dad's golf clubs at him and missed, thank God, or I could have killed him. It hit the wall and made a hole—more trouble for me.

My mother would get after him for making me angry because she knew he did it on purpose, so we would both get in trouble. Mom tried to tell me not to let him get to me, but occasionally he did. I guess I had a bit of a temper, but it only came out when he taunted me. You can see I wasn't perfect. It made me mad because he started it, but I got in trouble. I needed to learn some self-control. Dad didn't know about these things, or I probably would not be alive to tell my story.

Herb was quite a debater and to this day, no matter what the subject, he takes the opposite side. I find it challenging to have a conversation with him sometimes because I never know what he really believes.

Ken, whom I was closest to, was quieter and more reserved. He usually only had one friend at a time. Where we lived when I was in fourth grade, there was this massive group of bushes in the back yard, and in one area there was an opening, like a cave, where we would hide to get away from Dad. It was a private place where we sat together and talked until we felt comfortable going back in the house.

When I was eighteen, my brothers and I went our separate ways, and I didn't see or communicate with them again for about ten years. By then, we had developed into adults, and it was as if we did not know each other. We have never been close as adults, but they are family and always will be.

Ken was an alcoholic for twenty-five years. I believe that is how he hid from his past. He finally joined AA, and his wife and three kids went to Al-Anon. I am happy to say they are a close family today.

The only family member I felt a real connection to was my maternal grandmother, but I lost her when I was sixteen.

My Grandmother

August 8, 1959

Dearest Grandma,
Oh my God, I miss you so much. It's not fair, why you? It should have been him, or even me, but not you. You're the only one in the world who made me feel wanted. I need you.

I hate my father, he should have turned the wheel the other way, and then he'd be dead instead of you. He should have done something to save you.

Oh, God, what am I going to do without you?
I love you, Grandma.
Caroline

I remember my grandmother on my mother's side; she was short and round with a happy face. She was pleasant and loved by everyone. She was an artist, taught ceramics, and painted advertising signs and Christmas scenes in many store windows. She did oils, watercolors, and pastels. One time, the local paper did a whole page article featuring her.

I wish I could have spent more time with her, but moving as we did, our times together were few and short. However, we did get to spend one summer near her.

Mom and Dad rented a house not far from my grandparents' farm. It was wonderful and the best time of my life because Dad wasn't around much. My dad behaved himself when we visited my mother's family. There were too many witnesses. He made it clear that he felt that farmers were beneath him. He only tolerated them.

At home, when I was younger and felt overwhelmed with emotion and tears, I would sit on the floor in my closet. I would wrap my arms around my knees, lay my head down, and sob. My heart beat so hard that sometimes I could almost hear it. It was safe, quiet, and no one would bother me there. I would let the emotions run their course until I felt calm again.

At the farm, I would go down the lane where the cows were grazing and sit on a big rock and sing made up songs to the cows. Little by little, the cows would wander over out of curiosity, and I could reach up and touch their big soft noses.

Cows have such big sad eyes, which is why I liked them so much—I felt that sadness too. I felt alone and unloved. They made me feel wanted and they liked my singing, and if I sang, they would stay there, chewing their cud and watch me. I felt accepted by the cows. It was private, and no one else knew about it. It was something of my very own and safe like the closet.

My grandparents raised chickens and sold eggs. They had cows, but they rented most of their farmland to a nearby farmer. I learned to pluck a chicken at the farm. Yuck! First, Grandpa would grab one by the head, hold it on an up-ended log, and chop its head off with an ax. The body would run around headless for a while, and it was the weirdest thing I ever saw. Grandpa dipped them in hot water once they stopped moving, and we would pull the feathers off.

I played with my cousins and rode my bike all over the countryside. My cousins always had boxes of comic books, which my brothers and I devoured. We couldn't read comic books at home, as my father said they were low class. If we wanted to read, we could read a book.

I loved my grandmother very much. She was killed in an automobile accident on August 8, 1959, when I was sixteen. My parents, grandparents, younger brother, and I were coming home from my great grandfather's funeral, and a drunk hit us. It was about a two-hour drive from where we lived. We had visited with relatives and started home. Before we left town, we stopped so my mother could look up her cousin's phone number in a phone booth and call her. When my mother and grandmother got back in the car, my mom got in first, and grandma got in second, reversing the order they were sitting before.

I was sitting behind my dad, who was driving, my grandfather was in the middle, and my younger brother was behind my grandmother. My mother was in the middle of the front seat. We headed home at dusk down a two-lane asphalt country road. The street was damp from a slight mist. I looked up and saw a car in the distance driving toward us on our side of the street. Big ditches lined both sides of the road. The choices were to go into the ditch or move over into the oncoming lane. The ditch would not have been a good option. The shoulder was very narrow, and the ditch was deep, so chances are it would have resulted in injuries. There were no other cars on the road, so going into the other lane, if the other car didn't move, would have avoided injury. However, who can predict another person's actions?

My dad slowed down, stayed calm, and waited until the last minute to decide what to do. The other driver didn't move back into his lane, so my dad moved to the other lane.

Just then, the other driver became aware of where he was, and he moved too. With no time left for either of them to change lanes, Dad turned the steering wheel so we would not hit head-on. The driver-side front headlight of the other car impacted our passenger front fender. The cars wrapped around front to back, flew apart, and stopped about fifty feet from one another. Our big Chrysler looked like an accordion from one end to the other. The other car was old and just fell apart. The driver and passenger were thrown from the car and had minor injuries.

When I realized the two cars were going to hit, I think I passed out. I could feel the sensation of being thrown forward then backward, but I didn't see, hear, or feel anything. Weird! I don't know how much time passed before I became aware of things around me. It was enough time for several other cars and what seemed like many people to show up. They pointed their headlights toward our two cars, and it was almost like daylight. It was dark now, and that gave the police and the ambulance the light they needed to help everyone.

I believe I was the first one out of the car. After that, I don't remember the sequence of events clearly.

Dad managed to get out so my mother could also. Upon discovering a small fire in the engine, Dad got a fire extinguisher from the trunk, and put the fire out before he collapsed. He had a broken hip and pelvic bones—it was a wonder he could even stand, let alone walk. The steering wheel had broken in half and hit him in the face, damaging his nose.

Someone asked my mother if he could call someone for her, and she gave him her cousin's number—the one she had just looked up—from memory. All the family was notified. By the time they arrived home from my great grandfather's funeral, they had messages to return.

My mother had an injured arm and leg, but nothing was broken. I walked around the car to check on my grandmother. She didn't look hurt. I asked her if she was okay, and she said, "Don't worry about me. Make sure everyone else is okay." Later we learned that her injuries were mostly internal. She had many broken ribs, and her right foot was almost severed. When they moved her to the ambulance, the broken ribs shifted—one punctured her spleen and one her heart.

My grandfather had his front teeth knocked out and a broken leg. My younger brother looked awful. When they tried to take him out of the car, he said, "Don't you touch me."

"This might hurt, son, but we have to get you out of there," replied the ambulance driver.

His head had gone through the side window and back in again. His forehead was sliced from side to side, and there was a gash from the middle of his cheek to under his jawbone. There were many other facial wounds and cuts behind his ears. Every joint from his waist down was out of place, but it seemed nothing was broken. Even though the doctors got everything back in place the best they could, they said he might not walk right again.

I was the only one in the car who wasn't hurt. I had a small scratch on my cheek from my broken glasses, and a scratch on my leg. I was shook up but physically well.

I remember sitting by the nurse's station at the hospital while the doctors and nurses attended to my family. I looked up once, and a doctor was talking to someone I couldn't see. He glanced at me and then asked that person, "How was the older woman related to the others?"

How *was*, oh my God, how *was*. My grandmother was gone. She died before she reached the hospital. I started to sob, and a nurse sat with me and put her arm over my shoulder. She was so kind, and I really needed that right then. She showed me the kind of warmth I rarely experienced.

The story about my brother's recovery is interesting. We stayed on my great-aunt and uncle's farm while my dad was in the hospital. It was a while before they could transfer him to a hospital closer to home. One day my brother was lying on my aunt's bed reading a book. I could see him from where I was in the other room. His crutches were next to the bed. He had shorts on and suddenly became aware that a big spider was walking on his leg. Well, it was a farm, what did he expect? It startled him and he jumped off the bed and hit the floor hard. The doctor said he must have knocked the bones back where they belonged. My brother never used his crutches again, and walks fine to this day.

My grandmother's loss hit me hard. I didn't ever remember feeling loved or cared for except by her, and now she was gone. It was like the only good part of my life ended with her. I loved the farm, but we never visited again. My grandfather remarried and moved to another state.

We finally returned home and settled into a routine, but things would never be the same.

Everyday Life

1946-1956

Hello out there,
I love the Lake House. It is the best place in the world besides my grandma's farm. These few little memories of happiness are all that keep me going. They give me a break from my sadness and something to hope for.
Caroline

The memories of my early years are vague, but I do have a few good ones. Based on where we were living at the time, I must have been four. It was at the Lake House or cottage as we called it. I think my father had something to do with the construction, because we were there a lot while it was being built. After we moved in, I remember my dad throwing me over his shoulder like a bag of potatoes, running through the house, and tossing me down on my bed. I lay there in a fit of giggles while he tickled me. Hard to believe that was the same man who later abused me.

The lake was where I learned how to swim. We took our rowboat out to a raft in the middle of the lake. My mother tied a rope around my waist to keep me safe, and put me in the water—it was sink or swim. I learned fast how to stay above water. I loved the water and spent a lot of time swimming.

We lived at the lake house for a while, and I went to first grade there. We spent summers there until I was between fifth and sixth grade when we moved to Massachusetts. I loved being at the lake house mostly because my dad was gone a lot while we lived there. I think he was going to school.

My mother tells a story about the three of us kids making popcorn once when I was in second or third grade. Ken was popping it on the stove. Herb and I were anxiously waiting to get our hands into it. Ken decided to look and see what was going on inside the pan and took the lid off. Mom said when she heard us squealing, she came in, and there we were, squatted down on the floor with our hands over our heads, and popcorn flying everywhere.

Now my dad would not have seen the humor in that. Although when I think about it, I laugh. He probably would have punished us. Thank God he wasn't home.

I don't recall when the abuse started, but it was by the time I was in the third grade. I remember my mother telling me once that my dad hit Ken, my older brother, on the bottom and left a bruised handprint there when he was two. So, he was hitting Ken when I was a baby.

When I was in the fourth grade, I told my Sunday school teacher that I had a twin sister who lived with my grandmother on the farm because my parents didn't want us raised together. I don't think she believed me, and she told my parents. Oops! Caught! When I look back, I can understand why I did that. I put part of me in the place I most loved, on the farm with my grandmother.

When I was in the fifth grade, one day I stood in the bathroom soaking toilet paper and throwing it up into the air. I giggled with amazement that it stuck on the ceiling with a splat, never giving a thought to the terrible punishment this childish act would bring. Both my brothers had also done their share of sticking wet paper on the bathroom ceiling. It held well, but was difficult to get off when dry.

"All right," my father would say, as he lined the three of us up. "Which one of you threw the toilet paper on the ceiling in the bathroom?"

We stood in silence, knowing that whoever owned up to the task was going to be whipped.

"If no one admits to this, I'll just have to punish you all." That was his favorite thing, so either Ken or I would always confess. Ken and I would take turns taking the blame for things. It was not planned; it just happened that way. Herb, however, never took a turn, the little brat.

I think Dad enjoyed lining us up like that. Like Hitler getting ready to condemn us to death. Somehow, I think it gave him a sick sense of power. Oh, how I hated and feared him. Why, then, would I stick that paper on the ceiling if I knew it would bring pain and sorrow? Because I was just a kid.

When I was in sixth and seventh grade, my younger brother had a teddy bear named "Teddy," of all things. I had a doll named Rebecca. He used to bring Teddy into my room, and we would get cozy, and I would make up stories about Rebecca and Teddy and how happy they were and how beautiful life was. Since I had no love in my life, my fantasies were always about how wonderful love must be.

Hello world,

I bet you think life is good. Well, think again. Things are not always what they appear. Sometimes it looks like Dad wants things to be normal, but I never know when it will change. I wish there were a way to tell what was going to set him off. I'm tired of living in constant fear, not knowing what will happen next. Most of the time, I don't even know what I'm being punished for.

OUT OF DARKNESS, INTO THE LIGHT

I feel like giving up, but the moments of good make me keep hanging on, hoping it will change.
Caroline

My dad liked to entertain and would tell my mother he was having fourteen for dinner on a certain date. He never lifted a finger to help. My brothers and I would help, which was okay, I didn't mind. Everything had to be perfect, as he loved to show off.

Saturday was cleaning day. My dad reminded me of a foreman on a cattle drive. I could picture him with his whip: clean this, pick up that, do this, do that, and on it went until the house was clean and ready for his inspection. He loved to rule. All the while we were cleaning, he would recline on the sofa and listen to classical music.

Sundays were for church and Sunday dinner. My mother didn't go to church with us; she stayed home and fixed dinner. We had a nice dinner on Sundays. When we sat down to eat, my dad would place his fists on the table on either side of his plate and say, "A meal fit for a king." God, he made me sick. That big plastered on fake smile. Did he think we couldn't see through it?

Holidays were a joke. Dad would put on that stupid smile and act like everything was great. Thanksgiving, we would travel to his sister's home and have dinner there, then we would spend the night. I didn't mind my cousins, but my aunt and uncle were rather cold. I got the feeling they saw us the same way my father saw my mother's family—like we were a bunch of farmers.

At Christmas, we would decorate a tree. When Christmas morning came, you would have thought my dad was Santa Claus himself. He could switch between Mr. Nice Guy and Mr. Nasty so easily—confusing. Did he somehow think that made up for all the abuse?

My brothers would get annoyed with me on Christmas morning because I was always the last one up, and no one could open anything until we were all up. I certainly wasn't a child who was up at dawn looking for what Santa brought.

When we lived close enough, my mother's family would rent a hall up by the farm, and we would all meet there for a big Christmas potluck. There were many kids and lots of fun. I really liked that. I loved my mother's family; they were warm and friendly.

We would dye eggs on Easter. I never looked forward to the holidays. They didn't make me feel anything. They were just another day that made me worry that something I would do or say would set Dad off. All I wanted to do was hide in my bedroom. We looked like the perfect family, but were anything but.

Once, my dad took my bedroom door off because he said I didn't deserve any privacy. Mom eventually put it back on.

Hello, Is anyone there?

I hate dinnertime, sitting there listening while Dad lectures us about all sorts of things, and tells us how we don't measure up to his expectations. We aren't perfect and never will be.

"What did you do today?" he'd ask. It didn't matter what I said, I ended up being punished for something. Just being stupid and unattractive was enough reason.

Why doesn't Mom say something? I know it's my fault; I'm just not good enough. Why can't I be better, so he will like me? What's wrong with me, anyway? I hate myself.

Caroline

Usually, dinnertime wasn't a pleasant time, but Sundays were different. Weekdays we would sit down at the dinner table, and Dad would want to know all that went on that day. Punishment was dished out at the dinner table.

"Do you want it tonight after dinner, ten whacks, or tomorrow morning?" Of course, we always said "tomorrow," and hoped that he would forget. He never did.

Dad had graduated to using boards on us by this time. When I was in eighth grade, he would make us pick out a board, then set us on the bottom basement step to watch him cut a handle shape on one end of the board. Then, cool as a cucumber, he gave us our whacks. That was like double torture. This wasn't a pretty picture, but it was at least better than the times he lost control and lashed out violently.

My mother learned when we were little not to interfere when he was battering us because if she did, he became worse. He never hit her, but would hit us to punish her. She would never comfort us after he had his way with us. She never said a word.

High School

September 1957

Hello, can anyone hear me?

I hate school. I'm so stupid I never get anything right. I'm afraid of my teachers and afraid to ask questions. Dad's going to be so angry with me, but I can't help it. He tells me I'm an idiot, so what does he expect from me.

I thought I had some friends at last, and started to feel a little better, but they hatefully turned on me. My God, what's wrong with me? Why doesn't anyone like me? What do I do that causes this? Why did they shut me out? If I don't know why it's happening, how can I fix it? I hate myself. I must be worthless, or someone would like me. I wish I were dead.

Kay

During the school year, we had to stay home after school and do homework every day, even if we didn't have any. Of course, how stupid of me, we could always read a book. The one pleasure I had was writing stories. I kept them hidden; they were my secret. Most of them were about people who had a life different than mine. I even tried some mysteries. I loved Erle Stanley Gardner's books about Perry Mason and read them all. Maybe I was practicing for today.

The physical abuse was bad enough, but there was also the mental abuse. Dad never had a kind or supportive or constructive word for anyone in the family. We were an embarrassment to him, nothing but a bunch of farmers. He had no problem telling me all the time how stupid and unattractive I was. He was always telling me how to dress to cover up all the bad points and believe me, according to him, there were plenty. The boys couldn't roll the sleeves up on their long-sleeved shirts, as that was low class. If I wanted something on my head, it had to be a hat, as anything else was low class. He made me feel like I should hide from the world.

He was continually reinforcing my feelings of self-contempt. Once, when he was scolding me about something, I said, "But I thought—"

He stopped me and said, "Don't think, I'll tell you what to think."

When my older brother started high school, we moved again. My mother put her foot down this time and said, "These kids are going through high school in the same school. No more moving."

In the eighth grade, I started telling everyone my name was Kay. Before that, everyone called me by my first name, Caroline. I don't recall why I decided on Kay. I guess I thought that changing my name made me a different person. Now I was someone new.

I loved music class, and I liked to sing in the choir. The teacher asked me once if I wanted to do a solo, and I about fainted. You mean to stand up in front of everyone and sing? Not on your life.

I didn't do well in school and barely passed each grade. I could not take written tests but did better with verbal tests. This disturbed my dad because school business was his life, and I think he felt this made him look bad. He took me down to Wayne University and had me tested. My IQ was 132, which was above average, and this infuriated him.

"What's the matter with you?" he said with disgust.

I sat there in silence. *What? That cannot possibly be correct. I can't get anything right. He's right; I am stupid.*

He should have looked at himself. The way he treated me made me feel so bad about myself that I could barely function. I couldn't look anyone in the eye. I always walked with my head down, looking at the floor. I couldn't raise my hand in school to ask questions. I was afraid of my teachers. When I walked down the street, and someone was coming toward me on the same side, I would cross the road rather than pass them on the sidewalk. I was afraid of people.

I was never good at making friends. We moved so much it was hardly worth the effort. When I was in the ninth grade, there was a girl my age across the street, and I made friends with her. We started hanging around with the girl on the corner and another girl on the next block over. We were all in the same grade, the school was only two blocks away, and we all walked to school together. I felt like they liked me, and I belonged. We hung out on the weekends and after school when I could and did many things together.

Then one day, my "friend" across the street handed me an envelope and walked away. The letter told me that they did not want me in their group anymore. All three girls had signed it. It also said if I didn't know what a queer was, I should find out. I didn't understand what I had done. I never touched any of them. I thought we were all friends, and everything was fine. How could it go so wrong?

I cried for days. My mom tried to tell me to let it go and move on, but I couldn't. I wanted to know what happened but was afraid to confront them about it. None of them ever talked to me again.

They reconfirmed my belief that I was an awful, unlikeable person.

School went on, and for the next two years, I didn't let anyone close to me. How could I? It was just too risky.

After that, I started sneaking out of the house at night after everyone was asleep. I walked two blocks to the all-night Coney Island. I would sit there and drink a coke and listen to music on the jukebox. The song I remember most was "Mack the Knife." I have no idea why that sticks in my head, but it does. Most of the time, I was the only one in there, and sometimes the guy behind the counter would talk to me. I think many people thought I was stuck up because I was never able to start a conversation. I was anything but stuck up; it was more like stuck down. I was always afraid of doing or saying something stupid. Then the wrath of God would come down on me. Coney Island was my little secret, like the cows down the lane and my closet. It was my little getaway place.

Thank God I was never caught, unlike my older brother. He would also sneak out, push the car down the block and start it, and go who knows where. One night he came back, and someone else was parked where he needed to park so Mom wouldn't know her car had been moved. He got in trouble from Mom, but she never told Dad.

Sometimes after school, some of the kids would stop at the drugstore. On occasion, I would stop too. Back then, they had soda fountains in drug stores. We would all get a Coke, and they would start cutting up and kidding around and having fun. I would mostly watch, but sometimes I would try to join in, but always felt like a fish out of water. I didn't belong.

My younger brother stopped in one day while I was there. He was bringing home a big coffee can with white mice in it. He was supposed to take care of them for his class that weekend. The guy behind the counter said, "What you got in the can, kid?" He reached for the can, and somehow it fell over and the lid came off. What followed was the funniest thing I had ever seen. The girls were screaming, and the guys were running around trying to catch the mice. My brother was upset, and the guy behind the counter was hollering, "Get those things out of my store." I'm sure the poor mice were scared half to death. They gathered up all the mice, and everything settled back to normal, and we all went home.

In my senior year, I failed a required course on government and economics and had to go to summer school to make it up. They let me go through graduation anyway with an empty diploma folder. I barely passed the class in summer school, but they gave me my diploma. I had no idea what I was going to do with my life or where I would go. I would be lucky if I could even get a job. Why would anyone want to hire me?

Dad's Gone

June 1961

Dear Self,
 Why are you so upset; the jerk is gone, gone, gone. Oh well, I guess I do feel better. I'm happy for my mom. I hope the rest of her life is peaceful; she deserves it.
 I'm out on my own now, but I don't know what I'm going to do with my life. I don't have the brains to get a decent job. I got a job as a carhop. It was fun, and believe it or not, I started dating. I'm not feeling so hopeless right now. However, I don't know; something does not feel right with me.
Carol

I graduated and didn't want to go to college. Dad pulled some strings and got me in anyway, even though I had to take some remedial classes. I didn't understand him sometimes. Why would he care if I went to college?

Well, I went to college, and Parents' Day was coming up, and I'd be damned if I would tell them. I took every pill I could find in the dorm. I would show them Parents' Day. I made a feeble suicide attempt and ended up in the hospital having my stomach pumped. I was sent home and told I could not come back without a report from a psychiatrist.

My dad wouldn't come with my mom to pick me up from school. I wasn't surprised. However, he was waiting for me when I got home. He came into my room with contempt in his eyes and told me, "Don't you ever tell anyone what you did." He had no words of kindness, compassion, or concern. Of course not—I had just embarrassed him once again. Not only was I stupid, but I had also tried to kill myself. The college was out of town, and the people at home did not know anything about what happened—lucky him.

My older brother was married and in the service by the time I was eighteen, and my younger brother was still in high school. I was home from college and looking for a job.

One day my dad handed me two letters, one addressed to my mother and one to me, and told me he was off to Ohio to see about a new job. He asked me not to open either letter until my mother came home. He had talked her into visiting her sister for a few days, which was very unlike him. I was surprised my mom hadn't suspected something. Maybe she did, but I am sure what happened was not what she expected.

He needed time home alone so he could pack his things without her around. I only saw him put one suitcase into the car, but he took lots more because he knew he would not be back. He got into his car and backed out of the driveway. I knew he was not coming back.

So, why was I crying? Why was I so upset? Eighteen years of misery were over, and I should have been jumping for joy, but my last chance to win his love was gone. Even after all he had done, I still wanted his love. I had not learned yet that he wasn't capable of loving me, and it had nothing to do with me. He had a problem, but I didn't know that then.

I didn't have a good history of doing as I was told, so naturally, I opened the letter addressed to me as soon as he left. As I had already guessed, he was telling me he wasn't coming back. It started, "Your mother and I can no longer..." Everything after that was a blur, and I don't remember it.

I wasn't sure what to do, so I went to Pat's, our neighbor, who was a friend of my mother's. I showed her my letter, and she said I needed to call my mother. I called from her house, and when Mom answered, I started to cry and could not talk to her. I just handed the phone to Pat.

Pat read her my letter, and my mom asked her to open her letter and read it to her, which she did.

I heard Pat telling her to drive carefully, that we were fine, and there was no hurry for her to get home.

My most treasured wish had come true. Dad was gone. Why had he waited so long? It was too late to do me any good now. I was old enough to be on my own. I was traumatized and filled with hate and joy all at the same time.

When my mother got home, she started checking around to see if she could find my father. She called his secretary, Faith, and her husband, Bill, answered the phone. He said, "I don't know where your husband is, lady, but my wife is gone too." WOW! He asked if he could come over so they could talk. She said, "Okay." She asked me to stay at home; I guess she didn't want to be in the house alone with a strange man, especially under these circumstances.

What a meeting that was. Mom and Bill hashed over all the times my dad and Faith were at late business meetings and managed to go on business trips together. They discussed how naïve they must have been to not see what was going on. At one time, I remember seeing five cigarettes burning in the large ashtray in the middle of the table and only two people smoking. They were a mess. I guess under the circumstances, what else could you expect?

Their spouses had just deserted them without a word.

We should have all been glad he was gone, but the world as we knew it was crumbling. Everything was going to change. Nothing would ever be the same again. Of course, I was out of school, and my life was going to change anyway, but this was different.

We found out later the reason he left so quickly was that he had been caught doing something that wasn't legal or against the school rules. They knew about his affair with Faith and used that as leverage to get rid of him. They threatened him with exposure in the newspapers if he did not leave willingly. They paid him off, and he took Faith and left.

Several months later, Bill called my mom and said he had always bowled on a couple's league and wondered if she would like to be his bowling partner. She asked me what I thought, and I told her that she would probably have fun, since she liked to bowl too. He seemed like a very likable man, and she agreed to be his partner.

My dad and Faith moved to New Mexico, went to Mexico and got divorced from my mom and Bill, and were married and lived there in Silver City,

New Mexico. Mexican divorces were not legal in Michigan, so my mom and Bill both had to get divorces too.

Faith took all their money when she left, leaving Bill with nothing. She took the kids' college funds and all their savings. My dad did pretty much the same thing. Nevertheless, when Bill was trying to get his divorce, she wanted more. It took him three years because his lawyer died in the middle of everything, and a new lawyer had to start over again.

You will get a kick out of this. Sometime after my dad left, he contacted my mother and asked her to send him some things he had left behind. Just box them up and send them collect. I don't know if he contacted her personally or had someone else contact her. She got out an old wooden truck he had and packed it with all the junk she could find that was worthless and weighed a lot and sent it off. Way to go, Mom. Stick it to him.

I stayed with my mother for a while, but all we did was fight. It became unbearable for me, and I imagine for her too. We didn't see eye to eye on anything. She made us an appointment to see a therapist. I went a couple of times, and he told me nothing I did not already know. I don't know how long my mom went.

One day while she was at work, a friend of a friend with a pickup truck came over, and I took my bedroom set and enough items from our furnished basement to set up an apartment and left without even telling her I was going.

I was so full of anger that I didn't even see that I had just done the same thing as my dad, and she must have been devastated. I was gone six months before our next contact. I called my mother's sister one day, and she told me to call my mom, that she was very worried about me. I called, and we got together and made peace, and mended our relationship to the point where we could be civil to one another. The six months apart had given us both an opportunity to grow a little. I still couldn't move back home. I'd had a taste of freedom and wasn't ready to give it up.

By that time, my mom and Bill had become good friends. When his divorce was final, he asked her to marry him, and she did. They had a small wedding with close friends and us five kids—myself, my two brothers Ken and Herb, and Bill's kids John and Susan. We all got along, which was good. None of us wanted to have anything to do with the runaway spouses. As time went on, it just became a funny story to share with our friends. Our parents swapped partners.

After they got married, Bill said his house was big enough for all of us and wanted me to move in with them. Bill was easy to get along with and so funny. For sure, my mother and Bill got the better end of this swap. They were married about 38 years when Bill passed away. My mother lived another 13 years.

My life was like a soap opera. I didn't have a choice in my parents, but I did for other people, and just about every choice I made was a disaster. I picked all the wrong people. Like a broken record, I chose people who would use me and abuse me, and mess with my thinking, the same as my father. It was bad enough I had his voice running around in my head, telling me how bad and no good I was.

I was sad and depressed a lot, a textbook case of abuse, and looked for love in all the wrong places. My work life was perfect, and my personal life was a mess. I didn't know how to love and didn't know what it felt like to be loved. Because of that, I made many wrong choices regarding relationships.

I was out of school and on my own and it was time for me to forge out a place in the world. I was certainly unequipped to do it.

Don the Liar

August 1962

Hello out there, can you hear me?

I feel awful; everything is going wrong again. I had about a year of car hopping and running around looking for love. It wasn't bad, but it was going nowhere.

Going to see my dad was a stupid thing to do. He's no different but doesn't hit me anymore. He talks down to me all the time. I don't like Faith, Bill's ex-wife, and my dad's current wife.

I've started dating again, but I know I'm only being used as a drinking buddy and bed partner, but I'm taking what I can get. I just want to be close to someone. I want to be held.

Oh God, how could I stoop so low as to knowingly sleep with another woman's husband? I am the lowest of the low. That's what my dad did. How could you? Fern was my friend, and I betrayed her and slept with her husband. I knew it was wrong, and I did it anyway.

I met Don and thought I was in love. He took me in and lied to me, used me, and deserted me. Why would he do this to me? What is it about me that makes people think they can take advantage of me like that? Why am I so easily fooled? Why do I believe everyone's lies? What is wrong with me?

What can I expect? I'm useless; who would want me? He just wanted a bed partner while he was away from home. Guess that's all I'm good for. Why would he want someone so stupid and unattractive anyway? This is just what I deserved for sleeping with Fern's husband.

I am grateful that Bonnie helped me through this mess with Don.

I'm so depressed and unhappy. Where is my life going now?

Michele

When I was 19, I packed up my few belongings and took a bus to New Mexico. My dad and Faith lived in Silver City at that time. I was hoping something might change between us. Right! Sure, like he would suddenly love me. I stayed with them for a short time. While there, I never got the feeling that he cared if I was alive or dead. He just smiled a lot and put up with me. His actions always seemed so phony.

I took a typing class, and Dad got me a job at the university where he worked. That gave me some office experience.

He and Faith had lied to everyone. Their friends and co-workers thought they had five children and didn't know about the divorces. Well, I spilled the beans, which I thought was funny at the time.

I stayed until I couldn't take it anymore. Dad being nice and smiling all the time was hard for me to accept. Then I moved to Las Cruces, a small college town in New Mexico, with only fifty dollars in my pocket. The day I got there, I rented a room from a woman. The room was attached to her garage and had a big desk, a large dresser, a bed, and a bathroom with a shower. It was all I needed.

I went to the unemployment office and got a job the first day as a credit clerk at a Montgomery Ward catalog order house. The manager, Fern, took me under her wing and helped me get settled. She knew I was young and alone in a strange town.

I didn't have a car, but the town was small, and I could reach every place I needed to go on foot. There was a bar, Lapuma's, between home and work, and most nights, I never made it home without stopping. I wasn't of age, so I altered my driver's license to look like I was over twenty-one, but no one ever questioned my age.

When I started sleeping around, it was because in my mind, if they wanted me, it must mean they liked me. Not true, but I kept looking for the one who would actually like me. After a while, I knew we were not really friends, just drinking buddies and bed partners. But it was something, and I wasn't alone.

I started dating a young college professor. We spent more time at Toke's place than mine. He had a roommate, Blane, and we all did a lot of crazy things together. Sometimes on Sundays, we would even cross the border into Tijuana, Mexico.

I went to Mexico once with Toke and Blane and stayed for three days. We had not planned this stay, but things got out of control, and with everything there open twenty-four hours, it wasn't hard. I didn't show up for work Monday morning. When I did show up, it was late on Tuesday, and I was still a bit drunk. I got fired.

When I got back to my room, my dad and Faith were there. It seems when I didn't show up for work and didn't call, Fern went to my room and found my purse, which I hadn't taken because it wasn't safe to take it to Mexico. She saw my bed had not been slept in and got concerned and called my dad. I had listed his number for emergency contact, as he was the closest relative, but never expected it to be used.

I was surprised at my dad's quiet reaction. Faith took one look at me and said, "Well, what can you expect, look at her mother." She did not even know my mother. I didn't know what my dad had been telling her, but it wasn't true. I must have looked awful as I hadn't bathed in three days or had much sleep or changed my clothes.

"Look who's talking. At least she didn't run off with another woman's husband." I don't know where I got the gumption to say that, but I did. I suppose they were upset too. After all, they drove all the way there to find I was just dirty and drunk. Since they found out I was safe and alive, they just left. My dad suggested as they were leaving that I go talk to my boss and see if I could patch things up.

After I showered and got some sleep, I talked to Fern. I told her how awful I felt and was sorry, it was so unlike me and that it would never happen again. I got to Mexico and was with other people and had no way home. Well, she took me back. Of course, if she'd known I would end up sleeping with her husband, she might have considered doing something else, like wringing my neck.

I went out in the desert once and made love under the stars with Gordo, the bartender at Lapuma's. I saw him several times, but it was nothing, and I knew it from the beginning. After messing around with the grandson of the owner of the house where I rented the room, things got a little awkward there, so I moved into a regular furnished apartment.

After a while in the new apartment, I found my pay at the catalog order house wasn't enough, so I got a second job as a cashier at an all-night café that was owned by Fern's husband, Ray. I would get off work at Ward's at 5:00 pm and started work at the café at 6:00 and got off at midnight. I would go straight to the bar after work. One of the bars I went to was called The Cave. It was very nice and all underground, a cool place.

While I was working at the café, I started having an affair with Ray. At this time, I had stopped seeing the professor and Gordo altogether. Ray and I almost got caught in the act by a friend of his once while Fern was out of town. That slowed the relationship down. I only saw him occasionally now because he didn't want Fern to find out.

I met Don one night at the café when he and the guys he worked with stopped for dinner. We made a date for after work that night, and we went over to my place. Of all the guys so far, Don was the first I really liked. He was nineteen years older than me, but he didn't look or act it.

After a short while, he asked me to go to Albuquerque with him. His work crew had gotten a job up there. I told him I couldn't just leave my jobs like that and take off. He told me we'd get married when we got there. WOW! Get married? I didn't expect that since we hadn't known each other that long. I quit both my jobs with one day's notice, and off we went.

We moved into a furnished apartment, and I played at being a wife. After a while, he told me that because of a stipulation in his divorce, he could not get married again until his kids were eighteen years old. His youngest was fifteen, so we could get married in three years. What a blow. I might have gone with him anyway had I known, but he'd lied, and it took me by surprise. I felt it was too late to do anything about it then, and I was happy with him, so I just let it go, thinking we'd get married in three years. I told my family we were already married. We had fun, and I was having a good time playing house. I cooked and cleaned and did the laundry, just like any good wife would.

Don worked with cement, and the company he worked for was building an elevator shaft for a tall building. They poured the cement walls for the elevators, and sometimes I would go and watch the men work. Sometimes the guys would come over after work to have a few beers. They were funny, and I liked it when they came over, as they were the only company we had. This one guy, Ray, was really a riot; he could tell some of the funniest stories about Wall, North Dakota, where they came from. He would start the story, and the others would chime right in. I knew most of what they were saying couldn't possibly be true, but they were good at putting a story together on the spot as a team, and they made me laugh.

While we lived there, Don got letters from someone called Jay. He told me it was his uncle. He never shared anything he wrote with me—he just read them and put them away.

At the end of two months, they had finished their job in Albuquerque and were being sent to California. Don decided it would be better if he went ahead with the guys and got us a place, and then send for me. Since I knew no one in Albuquerque, he decided he'd drive me back to Las Cruces and drop me at the hotel there. We packed all our things (most of which were mine before I met him) in his car, and back to Las Cruces we went.

He got me settled in at the hotel, told me it would only be a few days, kissed me goodbye, and off he went. I never gave it a second thought, as I had no reason not to trust him. I only had sixteen dollars with me but could charge meals and drinks to my room. I felt that should be okay since he said he would send me some money right away.

I was lonely that night, so I decided to go to Lapuma's for a drink. On the way over, I remembered one day when Don and I were out for a ride, we drove past Ray's house. Don said Ray was married with three kids and his wife was expecting their fourth. She and the kids traveled with him on the job. So instead of going to the bar, I decided to go over and introduce myself. Their house was only about half a block from the bar. When I got there, there were several cars in the drive and a lot of people around, so I just walked by and went to the bar.

When I got there, Gordo wouldn't serve me because he said that Ray, Fern's husband, had come in after I left town and told everyone I was only nineteen years old. I showed him my altered ID, and he reluctantly served me, but made it clear it was the last drink I would get in there. I think Ray told him more than that I was nineteen. I drank slowly, trying to kill some time. No one talked to me, so I felt a little uncomfortable.

I finished my drink and started for the other Ray's house again. When I arrived this time, there were no cars around. It was dark, and I could see the lights on in the house. I went up to the side door. I knocked, and Bonnie, Ray's wife, answered the door.

"Are you Michele?" she asked before I could say anything. "The guys are out looking for you, they saw you walk by a while ago," she said.

"I saw you had company, so I went and had a drink at Lapuma's," I said. She offered me a soda, and we sat down at her kitchen table and started talking.

"You do know Don is married, don't you?" she asked.

"He told me he was divorced," I responded.

"Well, he's not. His wife, Jay, is my best friend," she said.

Jay was his wife? I was shocked. I had believed all his lies. I told her what he had said to me about the divorce agreement, and that the letters he was getting were from his Uncle Jay. I told her that we were to be married in three years and that he was going to send for me as soon as he got to California.

She said, "None of it is true, and he's not sending for you." She said she was ready to hate me because I was shacking up with her best friend's husband, but she thought something was funny when he showed up with all my things and was passing them out to anyone who wanted them just to get them out of his car. Now that she knew the truth, she couldn't hate me because I was an innocent victim of his lies; I had been taken advantage of.

I was devastated. What was I to do now? I had practically no money, a hotel bill I needed to pay, and I had been deserted.

When the guys got back to the house, Bonnie told them what Don had done. They were not aware of the extent of the lies he had told me. They thought I was just shacking up with him, knowing all the circumstances.

I was no angel; God knows I'd been sleeping around. But this was different. I hadn't expected anything from those other relationships, but I had from this one.

I went back to the hotel that evening and sat in the bar until I was utterly smashed, went to my room, and fell asleep. It sure didn't help a thing; when I woke in the morning, everything was still the same. I was still alone with no job, and in a hotel with no money to pay the bill. Boy, I'd really done it this time.

Well, I had to do it. I called my mother and told her I had been deserted. That Don had never divorced his first wife before he married me—a little white lie of my own. I told her what my circumstances were, and she was great. She wired me some money to pay my bills and live on until I got home.

I moved out of the hotel that night and moved in with Bonnie and Ray and the kids until it was time for me to leave. I was only with them for one week, but in that time, we became good friends. Finally, my train came, and I was on my way back to Michigan.

Little did I know that this was just the beginning of a whole string of bad choices I was going to make.

Jack the Alcoholic

January 1964

Hello, is anyone out there?

My God, I need help. I did it this time. Am I blind? Why can't I see these things coming? This guy's as big a mess as I am.

I wonder if I am being punished for sleeping around before I married him. He never wants anything to do with me. He is not affectionate or warm at all. Why did he marry me? I sure know how to pick 'um.

I'm pouring myself into my jobs. It's my only escape from what is going on at home. I don't want to be there anymore. I keep leaving him but can't seem to stay away. Oh, he makes promises to me, but after a while, I knew he couldn't keep them. Not that he doesn't want to, he just can't.

Michele

When I got back from New Mexico, I moved in with my mom. She had sold the house and was living in an apartment. We had a good time living there. She was dating Bill, and they were soon to be married, and I was sleeping around again. Being with family did not stop me as I thought it might. I think I fooled Mom and Bill, but I could have just been fooling myself. I told them lies about who I was with, and where I was.

I got a job at a nearby hospital in the billing office and got in with a group of single nurses and doctors that lived in the apartment building next to the hospital, and there was always a party going on.

After a while, I got a letter from a guy named Jack. He was Bonnie's brother. She had been talking to him about me, and he decided to write. Mom said not to bother writing back as he would not write again. I decided to write back anyway. He answered. He lived in California and was a surveyor. We corresponded regularly for about six months, and then he started calling, and we talked a lot.

One day he asked me to come to California and meet him. He said he would pay my plane fare and for a place to stay. I figured, WOW an all-expense paid vacation to California. I decided to go. My mother was not sure it was a good idea. I didn't blame her for being concerned, as I had been making many bad choices. But I mean really, what could go wrong? It was just a trip to California and back.

Just before it was time to leave, his company sent him to North Dakota on a job, so he changed my tickets, and I went to North Dakota.

He was not bad looking. His father was full-blooded Indian, and his mother was white. He got his looks from his father. He had Indian features, with a reddish-brown complexion.

I stayed with him in the motel where the rest of the crew was staying. I met his boss and the rest of the guys on the crew. He told me the night I got there that he did not want me to go back to Michigan, but to return to California with him where we could get married. Gee, once again, I thought someone loved me. He told the guys on his crew that we were getting married when we got back to California, so I figured this was the real thing. I let my mom know, and called my employer and told them I was not coming back and to mail my final paycheck.

The guys were drinking a lot, but that didn't seem unusual to me with them all being away from home. We were there several weeks. His boss asked him to drive the company vehicle back because his wife was sick, and he had to fly back home. So, we drove back and had a good time on the trip. We stopped in Wyoming on the way because it was western days there, and everyone had dressed accordingly and was having a great time.

When we arrived in California, we got married. Jack's boss and his wife stood up with us. The night we got married, he made love to me and said,

"There, that's the first time you've had it as Mrs. Horner."

He did not touch me again for many months. I asked him what was wrong. He said he was just tired all the time. I let it drop. I could count on both hands the number of times we had sex in the eight and a half years we were married. He did not have a problem before we got married, but once we were married, sex stopped.

I had not known him long enough in person to realize he was an alcoholic, or I would not have married him, although I'm not sure because I had never known an alcoholic and hadn't understood how it would affect our lives.

We struggled along. I got jobs and worked, he worked and drank, and I got used to it. I loved my jobs and enjoyed going to work. For a while, his job took him away from home during the week and home on the weekends. That was good too.

He became possessive and didn't want me to have friends unless it was as part of a relationship with a couple. When I would leave our apartment to go to the laundry room and stop along the way to talk to a neighbor, he would tell me to stop bothering the neighbors. If he thought I'd looked at or spoken to the bagger at the grocery store, he would say, "Stop flirting."

One day some friends of ours wanted to go out with us that night, and I told them we would. When Jack got home, I told him, and he looked all over the apartment and under the bed. Then he opened the freezer door and told me I needed to defrost the freezer before I went anywhere. I'd made sure the house was clean because I knew he would check.

There was maybe a quarter inch, at most, of frost in the freezer, not enough to make it worth defrosting. I started throwing the things from the freezer into the sink, and then on second thought, threw them back in the freezer and walked out.

Jack followed me and shouted, "Where do you think you are going?"

"If you want the freezer defrosted, do it yourself," I shouted back.

Our friends showed up that evening, and we went out with them. I won that battle.

Jack had been married before and about a year into our marriage, his eight-year-old son came to live with us. He had three children from that marriage. Bruce had a problem and needed special classes in school. They said he was trainable but not educable. His mother didn't want him around, and Jack didn't either. Bruce was a sweet kid, and I didn't mind having him around. He stayed with us until he was twelve.

It was sad that I couldn't leave Bruce at home with his father when I worked on Saturdays, because his dad would not even think to give the poor kid a sandwich for lunch. Some father he was. Therefore, Bruce went to work with me on Saturdays. He liked the pet shop I was working at then. What kid wouldn't?

I got a job as a bather at a Poodle Parlor, and they taught me how to groom dogs. I loved working with dogs. Jack and I had a motorcycle, and I used to ride it to work every day. It reminded me of riding a horse, which I used to do every chance I got when I was a teenager. It's such a freeing experience.

We lived in eleven different places while we were married. I left Jack seven times but went back each time when he promised he would quit drinking, which only lasted about two weeks each time.

While I was married to Jack, my dad called one Christmas Eve to tell me Faith had died. She had an asthma attack and died before they could get her to the hospital. Sorry, but I didn't feel bad for him at all. Did he expect my sympathy or something? I heard the emotion in his voice, which surprised me because I didn't think he had any feelings. I didn't know why he felt he had to call me. She was not my mother, and I did not care. That was his problem.

I got my start in banking while married to Jack. One day when I was in the bank, the manager started talking to me. I was looking for a job at the time. He said they didn't have any openings right then but would give me a call if one came up. I had not asked him about a job, since I didn't think I had the experience to work in a bank.

Well, this man came through for me. A week later, he called to tell me a teller had quit and offered me the job. He didn't even know if I could do the job. I never filled out an application or anything. I accepted his offer of employment and started the next day. I was surprised to find, after some training, that the job came quite easily. I had never done well in math at school but had no trouble at all picking this up. I did not know why this man did this for me, but I was grateful. It was the start of seventeen years in banking. I wasn't stupid after all. I picked it up easily and moved up quickly.

We moved once again, and I had to change jobs. I liked working at the bank, and I quickly got a job with another bank.

I remember my dad saying to me once, "If you can't say something nice, don't say anything." I don't remember in what context it was said, but it stuck with me. Because he said it, I was cautious when I thought about saying something not so nice. Maybe that was why I was not the same at work. I was happy, playful, and "nice." I was a very different person at work and after work with my co-workers.

Once, I left Jack after he went on a drunken rampage. I remember that day so clearly. What a confusing mess that night was. Bruce was not at home; he was visiting with Bonnie and her kids. It was a blessing he missed what happened.

Jack had been out drinking, as unusual. It had been going on night after night, and I'd just reached my limit.

I called my boss, who was also my friend, to see if I could spend the night at her house because I was leaving Jack. She said okay, so I packed my suitcase and waited for Jack to come home, because I didn't want to leave without telling him.

That night when Jack got home, what happened was almost unbelievable. When he saw my suitcase, he hollered, "Where do you think you're going?"

I told him I'd had it this time and I wasn't living with a drunk any longer.

"Okay, get out, who needs you."

I started to leave, and he stood in front of the door.

"You're not going anywhere."

"Let me out," I demanded.

"Okay, get out and don't let the door hit you on the way."

Again, I reached for the door, and as I did, he stood against the door and blocked my way. He grabbed the suitcase and pulled, and as this tug-a-war went on, we managed to get into Bruce's bedroom doorway, Jack pulling one way and me the other. All at once, I gave one big pull, Jack lost his grip, and I fell backward, and lost the suitcase. It bounced on Bruce's bed and went halfway through the closed bedroom window. I guess the breaking glass set Jack off because he started throwing things everywhere.

I managed to get to the kitchen and phone my boss, Rhonda. Her son answered, and just as I asked to speak with his mother, Jack took off his heavy work boots and threw one at me. His boot hit the ten-gallon fish aquarium on the kitchen counter, and it sounded like a gunshot.

The tank exploded—water, glass, fish, and gravel flew everywhere. I screamed and dropped the phone. By the time I got back to the phone, my boss's son had hung up and called the police. He and his mother were in the car on their way over to our house. In just a few minutes, there were four police cars in front of our house.

When the police officer came into the house, it was a wreck. All the books were off the bookcase, the lamps were on the floor, the coffee table was upside down, and so was the kitchen table. All the drawers in the kitchen were on the floor along with their contents, and the contents of the fish tank. The house looked like a cyclone had hit it. On top of that, a piece of flying glass had hit me on the cheek and made a small cut. Because there was blood on my face, it looked that much worse.

The officer said they usually did not get involved in domestic troubles unless someone's peace had been disturbed, and it sure looked like someone's peace had been disturbed. I went outside with one officer while another officer stayed inside with Jack. When I got outside, I was surprised at what I saw: Four police cars; all my neighbors; and my boss and her son getting out of their car. She ran over to see if I was okay. I explained that the noise that sounded like a gunshot was Jack's boot hitting the fish tank. My boss was relieved to hear that, but I think some of my neighbors were disappointed that it was not something more exciting.

The police asked if I wanted to press charges and I said, "No." All I wanted was to get out. If they would stay until I could retrieve my suitcase that was all I needed. They did, and I went home with Rhonda.

When we reached her house, I ran to the bathroom and throw up. By the next morning, I was calm enough to go to work.

Jack called several times, but I would not speak to him. Three days after the incident, I agreed to talk to him. He drove over to the bank. I went out, and we talked in the car.

He begged me not to let our marriage end this way. It was just too awful. He promised he would quit drinking. He said he loved me and did not want me to leave. After listening to him a while I finally gave in and said I would come back home, but I would not clean up the mess. He assured me that the mess had already been cleaned up. He had gotten a neighbor to do it. So, I went back to him once again, much to the surprise of several people, to try to make a bad marriage good. I kept hoping.

I could have never imagined what would happen next.

My Friend Susie

Summer 1972

Hello out there,
 I can't believe he did what he did. How sick is that? I almost lost my best friend over it. I feel awful.
 I guess my dad was right. I don't know how to use the brains God gave me. Not true; at last, I got a job now where I can use my brains, and my brain works just fine. Maybe not when it comes to my personal life, but it works quite well on the job.
 Now I'm alone and misbehaving again.
 Michele

We moved again, and I met Susie. She and her husband, Allen, lived in the apartment under us. She was nice looking and funny and a joy to be around.

I got a job with the bank there and quickly moved from head teller to assistant manager. Some of my friends and co-workers started calling me Mitch. I decided I liked it, so Mitch it was. When I was at work, I was a completely different person who laughed and had fun. While at work, it felt like that other "me" who was fearful, stupid, and unloved didn't exist.

Susie worked at a dry cleaner near us, and when an opening came up at the bank for a teller, I told her about it. She applied for the job and got it. It was fun working with her. We were always cutting up and doing things that made everyone laugh. One of the little skits we would do, when we had the right audience, that is, went like this. One of us would start.

"Susie, are you mad?"

"No."

"Are you sure you're not mad?"

"No, I'm not mad."

"You sure sound mad.

"Well, I'm not."

"Are you sure?"

"Okay, you just had to push it, now I'm mad. Are you happy?"

Susie was small-busted and was always making jokes about it. One morning, she told me that when she got up, she accidentally put her bra on backward, and it fit. She would say things like "my boobs look like sugar cookies with raisins on them," or "they look like fried eggs." We frequently met after work for a Pepsi and talked about what had happened at work. Sometimes some of the other girls at work would come too.

I remember well the incident that finally ended my marriage to Jack. It was bizarre and had nothing to do with his drinking. Even today, I wonder how something like that could have ever happened. Our marriage was never right; from the day we got married, it started downhill. I should have left him the first week, but I thought things would get better. But I was young and naive, and little did I know that things would do nothing but get worse.

It all started with an incident involving Susie and Allen, our best friends. One evening, we were visiting with them, and everyone but me had been drinking. They were not ready to call the evening quits, so they decided to go bowling. I was tired and Robbie, their three-year-old son, was in bed, so I said I would stay home with Robbie while they went bowling. Susie gave me a pillow and blanket, and I laid on the sofa and fell asleep. When they got home, I barely woke up and heard Susie say to let me sleep. She gave Jack a pillow to sleep on the other end of their big sectional sofa.

Around three in the morning, Jack woke me and said, "I can't sleep here. Let's go home." I got up and followed him out the door.

The following day, I called Susie to see what time she wanted us over as we had a barbecue planned for that day. Allen answered the phone and said

Susie was not feeling well, and let's cancel plans for today.

"What's the matter, did she have too much to drink last night?" I jokingly said.

"That's not it," he said. "She just isn't well."

I said, "Okay, I'll talk to her tomorrow at work."

As I started to hang up the phone, Allen said, "Wait, something happened last night, and we need to talk about it."

This is the story he told me. After they got home from bowling, Jack lay down on the sofa, and Susie and Allen went to bed. About three, Susie tried to wake Allen, which was not easy as he had been drinking and was sleeping quite soundly. When he finally woke and understood what she was saying, he ran out into the living room just in time to see us pulling out the driveway. He said if he had gotten there before we left, he would have killed Jack because he had just been in their bedroom with his hands under the covers, molesting Susie.

I could hardly believe what I was hearing. It must be a bad dream, it just couldn't be true, it was too bizarre. No one in their right mind would do a thing like that, drunk or sober. I hung up and sat there for what seemed like hours.

Could this possibly be true? Why would Allen and Susie make up a story like that? What did they have to gain by it? Nothing that I could see. The time seemed right: it was three o'clock when we left, and Allen said it happened around three. What was I to do? Our marriage had not been a good one, and now it was awful. I couldn't even think of getting into the same bed with him.

I slept on the sofa that night and went to work the following day. How did I face my best friend when this terrible thing had just happened with my husband? When I saw Susie, all I did was cry. We sat and talked about it for a while, and I believed her; it was just too bizarre not to be true. At first, she thought it was Allen but then realized it did not feel right. She sat up and saw Jack hurry out of their bedroom door.

I called my doctor and went in to see him after work. He was always easy to talk with, and I didn't know who else to call. He said I only had two choices. I had to make him face Susie with what happened. If he denied it and I stayed with him, I could never have another girlfriend as long as we were together. Or I could leave him.

That evening I gathered up all my courage and said, "Jack, I know what happened Saturday night."

He pleaded innocent. "What do you mean?"

"You know what I mean, about Susie."

"What about Susie?" he said.

"About you going into their bedroom before we left."

He continued to deny the whole thing repeatedly. When I suggested we go over and face Susie, to my surprise, he said, "Let's go."

I called, and when Allen answered the phone, I told him what the doctor had said and what had just happened and asked if he thought Susie could handle it. We hung up, and he talked to Susie. He called me back and said to come over.

We drove over, and when we walked in the door, Jack said, "What is this I'm being accused of?"

Susie screamed at him, "You know very well. What were you doing in our bedroom?"

"I don't remember anything like that happening," he responded.

I could see this was going to turn into a screaming match, so I pushed Jack toward the door and said, "Let's go." I looked at Susie with tears in my eyes and said I would talk to her later.

Jack and I drove home in silence, and when we got inside, he said again, "I don't remember anything like that happening."

"If you don't remember, Jack, you are sicker than I thought you were." We went to bed, him in the bedroom and me on the sofa, as it had been the last few nights.

I couldn't go to work the next day. I knew what I had to do, but doing it was another thing. The marriage was over; no turning back this time. I sat around and thought most of the day, and then three hours before it was time for him to come home from work, I started packing his clothes and all his things. We never had much, and most of what we had my mother had given us. I packed everything that was his or reminded me of him, and I destroyed all pictures of him.

When he got home, everything was by the door. I said, "It's over, here's your stuff. I'll keep one of the cars and talk to you in a few weeks about the titles."

He picked up his things, walked out the door without a word, his head hanging, and never looked back. He knew it was really over this time.

I filed for divorce *proper*, since I didn't have enough money for a lawyer. It only cost me $42.10. He never showed up for anything, and since we had no children and did not own a house, the divorce went through very quickly. I had no family in California, but I liked the weather there, so I decided to stay, at least for now, and see what happened next.

July 1971

Hello, is anyone out there?

My dad's voice is at work in my head again, telling me how stupid I was to get myself into such a mess with Jack, criticizing and belittling me.

I don't trust myself when I'm alone. I have no control. I have lived so long without any affection that I long for it. I need the loving touch of another human being. So once again, I am in the bars looking for some nice guy to pick me up. I'm no good. Why can't I stop this? You're nothing but a slut. I don't even like me, so how could anyone else.

I'm glad the people at work don't know about my personal life. They sure wouldn't respect or like me anymore.

Where am I going? Will this ever stop?
Michele

Jack was gone, and I was working hard at the bank every day. I was assistant manager now and was well-liked and respected by everyone. Gee, sounds like my dad; well-liked outside the house and a mess inside the house. *NO, I am not like him. Please, God, tell me I'm not like him, or am I?*

I started hanging out at night in a couple of bars and letting myself get picked up by what I thought were nice guys. In the year I stayed in California after my divorce from Jack, I had seven short relationships. They all ended friendly for various reasons. I found out one of the guys was married.

Then I met Rich. He was friendly, and we started seeing each other regularly. One night he called and wanted to go out. My friend Donna, one of the tellers at the bank, was at my apartment with a problem. I was trying to cheer her up. I told Rich, and he said, "Well bring her along, and we will cheer her up." I talked her into it, and the three of us went out. We had a great time, and when it was time to go home, Rich dropped me off first. I didn't give it a second thought.

The next day at work, Donna seemed a bit anxious and said she needed to talk to me. She and Rich had stayed up all night talking, and he had asked her to move in with him. I liked him but was not in love with him, so I told her that was fine; if they hit it off, I was happy for them.

We all stayed friends, and I started seeing Randy, one of my neighbors. The four of us had a lot of fun. However, that was not enough for me. Something was missing in my life. It had no purpose. Why was I here?

I was running around doing things I didn't feel right about but did them anyway. I didn't know how to stop and didn't like my life anymore. I got depressed; I was not the person that I wanted to be. Something was wrong, but I did not know how to fix it. I managed to keep my personal life separate from my work life. I couldn't jeopardize my job and that I knew. I was happy and upbeat at work, but after work, it was the pits.

So many people out there were having relationship problems. Just listen to the lyrics of songs. One that sticks in my head is "This Masquerade." The words brought tears to my eyes. I felt lost in a masquerade. I finally decided to move back to Michigan, where I had family. I thought with family around, I might behave myself. Little did I know what was coming next.

Darrow the Schizophrenic

July 1973

Hello world,
   At last, I'm really in love. I'm getting and giving all the affection and warmth I've always longed for. I feel cared about, and we are happy.
   This was a dream come true, and a couple years after wedded bless, we had a baby. Darchele. I couldn't be happier.
   Then things started to change. Little things at first, then they escalated as time went by.
                                    Michele

When I got back to Michigan, I moved in with Mom and Bill again and got a job at a bank. I decided I had to stop barhopping to find men, and joined a dating service. These services were a new thing in 1972. It cost me $1000, and I had to fill out a questionnaire with over six hundred questions on it. They investigated everyone who joined, to make sure they were not letting in people with criminal records, or other things like that. They matched people they thought would be compatible according to the answers on their questionnaires.

I dated a few men from the service, but none clicked until I met Darrow. He was good-looking, intelligent, and the conversation was non-stop. On our first date, he took me out dancing to a place where his parents liked to go. They were there, so I guess you could say we double dated with his parents the first time we went out. We had a good time. I got along with his parents, and I could tell they liked me.

I liked Darrow, and we saw each other every chance we got. He lived about forty-five minutes away, so it was not daily. I spent many weekends at his family's home.

I found out he had a medical retirement from the Navy. He was a Lieutenant Commander on a nuclear submarine. He had been diagnosed schizophrenic, paranoid with an eccentric personality. At the time we met, he seemed fine; everything appeared to be under control. When he joined the Navy, they enrolled him at Purdue University in an accelerated course in electronics. He was intellectually gifted and advanced quickly in the Navy.

He had been in about ten years when he had his first full-blown schizophrenic episode. He was in Washington DC having a briefing for a top-secret mission he and two others were going on. He walked out of the briefing, and it took the MPs three days to find him in DC, and enough thorazine to knock out an elephant to get him back to Bethesda Naval Hospital. He spent about six months there. They had to cancel the whole mission because of his knowledge about all sorts of classified information.

His mother always blamed the Navy for his problems, but that was not so. He had an aunt who had schizophrenia, and Darrow's doctor told me that he felt his father was borderline schizophrenic if there was such a thing. His dad was a little odd but not *schizophrenic* odd that I could see, but I'm no doctor.

We had only known each other for a few months when I invited him to my younger brother's wedding. That night he asked me to marry him. I should have known better, since I'd married Jack after only knowing him in person for a short while, and that turned out bad. I should have waited to marry Darrow, but I didn't. I felt he deserved a chance.

I checked with his psychiatrist, who said he was doing fine and marriage might be good for him, so I took a chance. We had a small wedding at his parents' home and took family and a few friends out to dinner at a nice restaurant afterward.

He wasn't working at the time, but I didn't see that as a problem. He had an income from his Navy retirement, so we had no problem waiting for him to find a job. He got a job less than a year after we were married, with a big corporation designing control systems for nuclear power plants. (Not bad!)

The first year was the best year of my life. I thought I had finally found heaven. We had such fun together. We would talk for hours on end about all sorts of things. I learned so much from him. He was like a walking encyclopedia. He was loving, affectionate, and not afraid to show it. Life was perfect.

Darrow was the opposite of Jack when it came to sex. Jack didn't want it, and Darrow had to have it every day and more if he could get away with it. I don't know which was worse. With Jack, I felt like I wanted it all the time because I wasn't getting any. And because Darrow wanted it all the time, I never had a chance to desire it.

Then it happened. Darrow had his first schizophrenic episode since I had known him. Every year Darrow went for an evaluation on his condition, which required him to travel to a naval base. I never gave it a second thought. The day after he got home, I noticed that he wasn't talking quite right, saying things that didn't make sense. The next day when he was supposed to be at work, he showed up at the bank where I worked and was still talking nonsense. My boss said to get him out of the lobby. I took him to the lounge down in the basement, then went upstairs to balance my cash drawer so I could leave.

We had two cars, so I followed him home. He was driving very slowly, and I could see he was talking to himself. Thank heavens he stayed off the main streets and took the back roads home. At one point, he even stopped the car to talk a while. He shouted something out the window and eventually started up again. I didn't interfere with him. I just stayed close.

Having never witnessed something like this before I called his parents for advice. Since it was a weekend, they suggested I bring him to their home until Monday. Then we could take him to the VA hospital, where they were monitoring his medications. That was a night to remember.

Dealing with him at that point was like dealing with an obedient child. He didn't think about what we were saying to him; he just responded. He was off in his own world and responding to suggestions from this reality. I said, "Darrow, change your clothes," and he continued talking in his little world while changing his clothes. "Come on, let's go," I said, and he just followed me to the car, talking all the while.

I wasn't too upset at this point. I was amazed and fascinated by what was happening. Could this be real? It seemed like a game he was playing, and he included me.

Off to his parents' house, we went. When we got there, everything proceeded as usual with Darrow walking around still talking nonsense. We tried to get him to eat with very little success. Not that he did or didn't want to, but his thoughts were somewhere else; he would start and then forget. We tried to get him to lie down and sleep, with the same results. He would lay down for a few minutes, and the next thing I knew he was up pacing around talking to himself again. I don't know what was going on in his mind. It certainly had nothing to do with what was going on in the rest of the room.

Oh, Darrow, where are you, talk to me. At one point when we were out of sight of the others, I grabbed him by the shoulders, shook him, and said, "Come on, Darrow, straighten up and act right." It had no effect. Now I started to worry. We called the hospital, and they said if it was an emergency to bring him in now, otherwise bring him in Monday morning. We decided that since his life was not in danger, it was not an emergency. We found out later that this condition is considered a psychiatric emergency, and we should have taken him in right away.

OUT OF DARKNESS, INTO THE LIGHT

There were three exits in his parents' house, and we each took an exit, and slept the night there in a comfortable chair. His mother told me he had once wandered off in that condition and ended up in a police station about two hundred miles from home. He had hitchhiked and scared some people half to death with his crazy talk. He voluntarily signed himself into the VA hospital in the town where the police picked him up. He spent a couple of weeks there and was released.

We went on the rest of the weekend as though nothing were wrong. We just kept an eye on Darrow so he would not wander off. When he went outside, we would call him back in, and he would obey. If we said, "Sit down and eat," he would sit down, eat two or three bites, and forget what he was doing again.

The weekend ended, and we drove Darrow to the veteran's hospital. He signed himself in as if it were the natural thing to do. We went up to the seventh floor, where a male nurse came to a locked door and took Darrow by the hand to take him into the ward. At this point for the first time since this started, he slipped into reality for a moment. He grabbed my hand and wouldn't let go. As the nurse pulled him away, he called out to me, "Don't leave me." That was all it took, and I was an emotional mess. I cried for two days.

He had been so well for so long that he'd decided he did not need his meds anymore. He was wrong. How could this happen to someone so intelligent? Somehow, it just didn't seem fair. They got him back on his meds, and everything seemed to go back to normal. He was home again in two weeks.

February 6, 1975

Hello world,
I have a baby. WOW, I can hardly believe it. A baby.
The day Darchele was born, I started crying and haven't stopped since. All the emotion that seemed to have faded away after Dad left was back. But, that's okay, I have a baby, someone to cherish and love and hold. I will love her unconditionally all the days of her life.
It was a rough start, but we made it through it. A baby, I cannot get my head around it. Is this real?
Oh, my God, I hit her. I will not be my father. NO, no, no. I swear, I will never hit her again. Never!
Michele

I wanted to have a baby. We were both tested, and they found that we both had problems, and we might have a one percent chance of ever conceiving. We went through the adoption process, but they discovered his mental condition and turned us down. It is funny that the day after they turned us down, I found out I was pregnant. That one percent chance came through.

Because I'd had many female problems since I was fourteen, and I was now thirty-two, the doctor expected I might have issues with the pregnancy. As it turned out, I didn't have any problems, and the delivery was normal. We had a girl, and combined our names and called her Darchele.

When she was born, it was the happiest time of my life. I had always wanted a child, and the picture I had in my mind was nothing short of heaven. It wasn't long after having her before I realized I was not in heaven.

I had natural childbirth and wanted everything natural, so was nursing as well. I nursed for two months, but my skin was so sensitive that it hurt. Darchele could sense my stress and would cry when she was near me. Darrow could take her and walk away, and she was fine.

When my doctor found out, he said, "Why are you doing this? It is not good for either of you. You get that child on a bottle right now."

I did, and everything changed. She no longer cried when she was with me. Thank God.

When Darchele was about two months old, Darrow got angry with me and threw a cup of coffee at me while I was holding her, which missed her head by only inches. That was the first time I had ever seen his anger. This was the beginning of the end, although I didn't know it at the time. That ending took about three years. I never dreamed it could go from this to something much worse. Things were changing with Darrow and I was worried.

When Darchele was about five months old, she was crying, and nothing I could do seemed to soothe her. She was fed and dry, her temperature was normal, and I couldn't see anything wrong. I became so frustrated that I lost it and hit her on the bottom. Of course, there was a thick diaper on her, so I didn't damage her in any way, but she was so shocked that she stopped crying. However, when I realized what I'd done, I couldn't believe it. Oh, my God! How could I do that? She was just a baby. *I am just like my father!* Oh, my God!

I ran to the phone and called Darrow's doctor. Thank God he was not with a patient, and his receptionist put me through. I was in tears trying to tell him what I had done and how awful I was. He calmed me down and assured me I was not a bad mother, and the fact that I called him was proof of that. I'd had a moment, and Darchele was not hurt. I picked her up and rocked her until we were both calm.

Divorced Darrow

Dear God,

How could you let this happen? If you're out there, please tell me how to fix this. I love this man. I need this man. I want this man. How can I help him? I want him to be okay. I cry for him a lot when I'm alone. I know this is going to end, and it's breaking my heart.

Sometimes he scares me now, but I know that's not the real him; it's the sickness. What can I do? Why is this happening to us?

I took a chance when I married Darrow, and it didn't work out. I am so sad, and I miss him, but I have a child to care for, and I can't take chances with her. So, to protect her, I need to give him up. It is hard, and I don't want to do it. Sometimes I long for the man I married, for his affection and warmth.

I shouldn't have married him, but if I hadn't, I would not have Darchele, and I'd be all alone. She gives me a reason for living.

"Young lady, you don't deserve any happiness. You haven't earned it yet."

"Daddy, get out of my head and leave me alone."

Earned it! How do I earn it? What do I have to do?

MICHELE FRANTZ

I WANT DARROW BACK. Please, I need him. God, please don't do this to me.
Michele

I think sharing me with Darchele disturbed Darrow. I'm not sure. I don't even know if either of us knew what was happening. He started having more and more episodes and stays in the hospital. Over the next three years, they kept getting closer and closer together. He would override his medications, so they kept changing his meds. One gave him the symptoms of Parkinson's, so they had to add another one to counteract those symptoms so he could function. Most of the time, it only took them about two weeks to get him back to normal. Sometimes it was longer. I asked his employer one day why they kept taking him back. He told me that when he had his feet on the ground, he was brilliant, the brightest employee they had.

Darrow's sickness focused on outer space. He was building an electronics lab on the upper level of his parents' garage. He said that we would never have reasonable space travel until we came up with a way to travel that didn't require fuel of any sort. He had an idea about something that ran with magnets and a Mobius strip.

He would tell people about Major June and Colonel Omar. They were from some other planet. She was a green-skinned woman with black hair and emerald green eyes, and he had silver skin and large round eyes that functioned independently like a bug. He said when he was with them, then he would be home.

When he would tell someone how to get to his house, he would say, "I live on a ball that is not a ball. I live in a hand that is not a hand. I live next to a stone, that is not a stone, and on a mountain, that is not a mountain, and on haven that is not heaven."

It made perfect sense if you knew what it all meant. Darrow lived on earth (ball), in Michigan (hand), next to Flint Michigan (stone), in the town of Mount Morris (mountain), on Haven Street (heaven). I wish I could remember all the things he used to say, but when things do not make sense, it is hard to remember them.

When Darchele was three, he had a bad episode. He needed treatment, and his parents and I had him committed to the state hospital because he would not sign himself in at the VA. He was out of control this time, and not obeying like a child anymore.

Darchele had just had her tonsils out, and my mother had her at her house. This way, I could work and deal with her father, who was in the hospital again. He had been there a while, and they called me to come and get him. It usually took a couple of weeks to get his feet back on the ground and start acting "normal" again—however, this time, I had my doubts. I had been to see him every day, and something didn't seem right, but who was I to doubt the doctors.

I drove to the hospital after work that day and went up to sign him out. He seemed to be fine, but still, I didn't feel right. We walked down to the car, and when he shut the door, he started talking nonsense again. I knew he wasn't ready to be released but was afraid to suggest going back into the hospital. By the things he was saying, I could tell that he felt good about being out and was determined not to go back. People with his type of schizophrenia could be sly at times to get what they want. It seemed for some reason he wanted out bad enough to fake wellness and got what he wanted. He just acted the way he thought they wanted him to, so they would release him. I drove home thinking that once I got him home, he would settle down. It didn't happen.

Fortunately, Darchele was still with her grandmother, so I didn't have to worry about her while dealing with her father. He talked non-stop until bedtime. Once, he said, "You are either number one or number two; either way one of you is going to die." The only thing I could figure was he was getting me confused with his first wife, whom he used to hit.

When we went to bed that night, he wanted sex even though I was reluctant. While making "love" to me, he spoke as though he was teaching the fourteen-year-old daughter of a friend of ours. He called me by her name and assured me that there was nothing wrong with what we were doing. I didn't say anything while this was going on because I was afraid of how he would respond. I just let him finish. He'd never hurt me before, but because of some of the things he was saying, I feared he might. You never know with someone who is not in their right mind.

When he finished, he realized what he'd done and became angry with me for not stopping him. I told him I was afraid. He couldn't understand why I'd be frightened. He doubled up his fist, and I thought, oh God, here it comes. Instead of hitting me, he turned and hit the bed stand with such force, it broke into three pieces, and a bit of wood went into the back of his hand. I could tell it was serious. With him being more concerned with his hand at the moment, he seemed to straighten up. We dressed and got in the car, and off to the hospital we went. We got there around midnight.

I was sitting in the waiting room, and I will never forget how I felt. There was an award show on television. Debbie Boone was singing "You Light Up My Life," and I just sobbed. I was thinking about how much I cared about this man when he had his head on straight. I knew that I had to do something, as he was getting worse and worse all the time. I couldn't raise our daughter with him. She was smart for her age and was repeating some of the crazy things he was saying. Thank God she wasn't home to witness all of this.

Of course, it was the middle of the night, and most of the hospital staff had gone home. The nurse came out and asked me if my husband had a problem. I said, "Yes." She asked me if I would come and sit with him, because they had to call in a vascular surgeon to take care of his hand. She said he'd damaged a tendon, and if they didn't take care of it properly, it could affect the use of his hand for the rest of his life.

Of course, I knew what the problem was; he was talking nonsense again. I explained the situation and agreed to stay with him. When we left the hospital, he seemed to have settled down and was quite tired from the ordeal and the meds they gave him. I was fearful and guarded, and I wasn't sure if I could trust him.

When we got ready for bed again that night, I put my clothes on the floor of my closet in one spot, in case I had to leave in a hurry. I was frightened, as he had been saying many scary things. I just wasn't sure about anything. I had never felt like this before with him. He was now acting differently, and I didn't feel safe anymore.

I lay in bed with my heart pounding, listening to him talk. He talked about things, such as how he felt it was okay for an adult to make love to a minor if he did not force them. He seemed to think all you had to do was convince them it was okay. I didn't say much, except that I didn't believe it was right. I just let him talk until he seemed to stop and fall asleep.

I didn't go to sleep. I waited until I thought Darrow was sound asleep and slipped off the side of the bed and groped around in the dark for my clothes and shoes. I went into the bathroom and got dressed.

When I came out of the bathroom and started down the stairs, I heard his voice behind me saying, "Where are you going?"

My heart about jumped out of my chest. What now? I told him I couldn't sleep and was going out to get a Coke somewhere.

"I'll go with you," he said.

"No, please, I need to be alone for a while."

"Please don't leave. You are my queen, and I know if you leave, you'll never come back."

I wasn't sure what would happen when I went through that door. Not sure where I would go or if I would be back. I only knew I had to take the first step, and walk through the door. I picked up my coat and purse and walked out with my heart breaking.

I got in the car and started driving slowly, tears streaming down my cheeks, wondering what to do next. I somehow knew that this was the end of our marriage. His episodes had been coming more and more frequently over the last year. He was spending as much time in the hospital as out.

It was the middle of the night, and I didn't know where to go at first. I didn't want to go too far. I had to decide what I was going to do. I only had one friend, Marlene; because of Darrow's illness, it was difficult to make friends. Even though I hated to impose on people in the middle of the night, I was sure my friend and her husband would understand, because they knew Darrow's condition.

I drove twenty miles to the nearby town where they lived. Of course, Marlene let me know that she knew something awful must have happened. I told her Darchele was fine and at my mother's and was safe, so she knew that was not a problem. Marlene made some tea, and I started telling her the story of how I ended up on her doorstep. Of course, I didn't tell her it was her daughter who Darrow thought he'd made love to that night.

I had to find out what was happening at the house, so I called to see how he was. I tried to talk him into signing himself in at the VA, and he said, "No," he would not do that ever again. He told me he was going to burn down the house and let it burn around him. I then called the neighbors to put them on alert. At this point, I did not know how much was talk or if he might actually do something.

I was cold, as much to do with the weather as my mental state. Marlene got me a blanket, and I remember rocking in a chair with that blanket around me, thinking about a song Darrow used to sing all the time. "What you going to do with a drunken sailor." Marlene knew he liked that song, so when I started singing "What you going to do with a crazy sailor," she almost laughed.

Not long after that, I called again to see what was going on. Darrow was hung up on the number three. He said he had already buried one kid in the backyard; did he have to bury two more? I was sure it wasn't a child he buried. I decided it was time to call his parents. After explaining the situation, even his mother said she didn't trust him. His dad said he would get his brother, who wasn't afraid of Darrow, and they would come and help.

It took them an hour and fifteen minutes to get there. My mother-in-law stayed with me at Marlene's because I was afraid to go back to the house. Darrow's dad and brother went to the house to see him. After talking with him a while, they could see he needed to be in the hospital where he could get some help, but he was determined to stay out and felt he was fine.

His brother and Dad came back to Marlene's to discuss the situation. We called the hospital, got hold of his doctor, and found that if he were unwilling to sign himself in, we would need a court order to have him committed at the state institution since the VA was a voluntary hospital.

When morning came, I stopped at work to let them know I was having a problem at home. Darrow's parents and I were at the courthouse when the doors opened. Things moved relatively fast, mainly because his parents were with me, and it wasn't just an angry wife trying to commit her husband.

After filling out all their forms and speaking with a psychologist, all three of us had to go before the judge and state, "Yes, we do believe that Darrow is mentally ill." I will never forget how difficult it was for his father to say that. It was the first time he had admitted to himself or anyone that his son was mentally ill, and he broke down and cried. Of course, we were all upset, but he seemed to take it especially hard.

Commitment is a very drastic step to take, and I felt that it would for sure be the end of our marriage if I signed that paper. If there was any hope left at all, signing this paper ended it. But, sign it, I must, because I felt at that time, it was the only right thing to do. I was glad that his parents were with me because they assured me I was doing the right thing.

Usually, they get a psychiatrist to go to the house and evaluate the situation, but because his parents were there with me and told them about his history, the judge gave us the court order. We took it to the police station and followed the police car to the house.

They asked if he had any weapons, and I said only kitchen knives. They asked if we felt he would be violent. I said I didn't know; he could be angry or just walk out and get in the car.

I couldn't go to the house and watch his face when they took him away, so his parents and I watched from the car down the street. He looked very calm when he came out. He looked like he had cleaned up and was ready for them, as though he knew something was going to happen. I thought, "He will never forgive me for this."

After they drove away, we went to the house to get some of his clothes and things he would need at the hospital. Through the door wall, I saw a shovel sticking out of the ground in the backyard. My thoughts raced back to my earlier conversation with Darrow. His father told his mother and me to stay in the house, and he went out to see what it was. When he came back in, I had to laugh, more out of relief than anything else. It was just his Mr. Spock doll he had buried, his favorite character from Star Trek. I had gotten it for him the Christmas before, just to be funny.

With great relief, we got in the car and headed for the State Hospital to drop off his clothes and see the doctor. The police were still there, and we talked with them. They said they were driving sixty, and he talked ninety all the way there about weird stuff. He told them many bizarre things.

He told the doctor many strange things too. Among them, he explained that he was not human, that he was a mixture of colored gases trapped in a human body (straight out of Star Trek).

They can't give him any medications on a commitment order while being evaluated; I think it was seventy-two hours. I visited him after the evaluation, and he treated me well. He seemed to have settled down a lot. He was more upset with his parents than he was with me. After a few days, he agreed to sign in at the VA voluntarily, so they let me drive him there. I was a bit apprehensive, since the last time I picked him up at the hospital, it didn't turn out well. However, the ride to the VA was uneventful.

Between the state hospital and the VA, he was in about a month this time. It gave me a lot of time to think and make up my mind. I had to protect my daughter. I couldn't have her growing up with his influence. With him around her, life would never be normal.

After he was home and settled in, I told him I was going to get a divorce. I couldn't take it any longer. He didn't fight it; he never even came to court. We sold our home, paid off all our bills, split the profit, and parted ways. It was sad because it wasn't that I didn't love him anymore. I just longed for a normal life for Darchele and me.

My one regret is that Darchele never knew the man I married. I don't think she has any memory of the loving, affectionate man I knew. I wish I could somehow give that to her. When she was little, he played with her, and it was touching to watch. I'm glad I have some pictures of them together showing the loving, affectionate man he was.

I wish Darrow hadn't been sick, as he was so interesting, and I cared for him. He was so smart; how could this happen?

Even at three and a half, Darchele understood her father's illness. She told me one day, "My daddy talks in two voices." I was amazed; so young, and she could see the differences in him.

Darchele was smart like her dad and used words that I thought she couldn't understand. One day she told me, "My grandpa's ridiculous."

"You don't even know what that means."

"Yes, I do; it means he's silly." She loved her Grandpa Bill. He always made her laugh.

It took Darrow about two years to let go. Sometimes he thought we were still married. He eventually accepted the divorce and went on with his life.

I was single again. Could I make a decent life for Darchele and me? Only time would tell.

Home Again

November 1979

Hello, Anyone out there?

I want you to know that my relationship with Darrow has changed something in me. I've had a taste of love but lost it. Now I am not sure what is happening to me, or what it is I want in life.

I've started drinking too much, and this is new to me. My banking years are ending. I want out of the public eye.

I'm doing some sleeping around, but it just doesn't do anything for me anymore. I am kind of numb and don't know what is happening to me. I only know I am sinking into a dark place where I don't want to be. I am feeling hopeless again.

I am seeing a psychiatrist now, and it helps me get through the week, but it's not enough.

Oh, what have I done to you, Darchele? My fear of abusing you has not allowed me to discipline you, and I don't like who you have become. I need to do something to turn this around. I know you are shocked to think I could say, "No," or try to tell you what to do, but it must be done. I can't let you go on like this.

Just as I thought things were getting better, Darchele's father entered the picture again. How could he do it, she was his daughter.

Michele

When I left Darrow, I once again moved in with my parents until we could get settled. Darchele was almost four. In about six months, the divorce was final. According to the divorce, Darrow could only see Darchele when there was another adult present.

I got a job at a bank, and I started going out a lot drinking with the girls. This became a way of life for me for about three and a half years.

After a while on my new job, I knew this wasn't what I wanted anymore. After seventeen years in banking, I was through. I didn't want to work with the public anymore. I was tired of dealing with people. I tried to transfer to an internal job at the bank away from the public, but they didn't have any available at the time.

I was the assistant manager at the bank. The manager said if I wanted to look elsewhere, she would give me time off for interviews. She was accommodating and understanding. It took six months, but I finally found another job at Bear Kat Products.

When Darchele was five, I realized I had been letting her get away with everything. I was afraid to discipline her for fear I would lose control and hurt her. Consequently, she ruled her existence. She was undisciplined and selfish. If you had something she wanted, she would bite your hand or arm until you let go. Most of the time, I didn't even like her. I had created a monster.

It was not all bad; we did have some good times. There was always hugging and affection between us when we were not at war with each other. I knew I had to do something, but I didn't know where to begin.

Having been an abused child, I was determined I would not abuse my child. As determined as I was, that didn't stop the abuse, it only changed its form. I abused her by ignoring her when she needed correction and letting her grow up without limits and controls by giving in to her every whim.

When I started to put my foot down and enforce some rules in our house, my daughter went into a state of shock. The next five years were awful. It was a battle of wills, and the fights were unbelievable. There were times when I would have to physically hold her down because she was going to hit me, and I wasn't about to let that happen.

What a mess. There were times when I felt the situation was hopeless. I blamed myself, and the more I tried to fix it, the worse the problem became, but I couldn't give up; there had to be a way to put this right.

We were living a lie. The public saw the perfect mother and daughter. She had learned how to behave in public, but I must give my mother credit for that. For that, I was grateful; at least the rest of the world wasn't seeing her through my eyes. However, out of sight of the rest of the world, the battle was still on. It reminded me of when I was growing up, and the world thought we were the perfect family, but that was anything but the truth. It was very different.

When Darchele went into second grade, my mother and Bill moved down south to Arkansas when Bill retired. We moved into our own apartment closer to my new job. The going out drinking turned into staying home drinking since Mom and Bill were no longer there to babysit Darchele, and I couldn't afford a sitter.

I had started seeing a psychiatrist while with Mom and Bill. I was so screwed up, and having all kinds of awful thoughts. I was again at that point where I didn't like myself, and my life had no purpose, no reason. I knew I had to get help because I had a daughter to raise.

I almost gave up. I was tired of making believe everything was fine when I had all these awful thoughts inside my head. Sometimes I feared that I had said things I was thinking out loud.

I lost my desire to eat and sleep. The only important thing for the moment was what I was thinking. I drank vodka and orange juice from the time I got home from work until I fell into bed exhausted.

I started to lose weight. That wasn't too bad since I was overweight, but I lost way too much. My weight had been on a five-year cycle. Five years up, and five years down, and this went on for many years. I'm not talking twenty or thirty pounds; it was over a one-hundred-pound fluctuation. I think I used it as protection from men. I thought who wants to date a fat girl?

The only thing that kept me from slipping all the way out was Darchele. Of course, she knew I was drinking a little, but that was all. She was only eight, and her bedtime was still 8 o'clock. She didn't have a clue what I was going through, and that was good.

Everything seemed so hopeless. It was as if I was doing it all on purpose but couldn't do anything to stop it. Like I didn't want to get better. I just wanted to slip into a hole and let the world pass by. It didn't want me, and I didn't want it. It would have been so easy at that point to let go, but I just couldn't because I loved Darchele. I had to straighten up. How would Darchele survive with two unstable parents? How unfair to her.

It seemed like if I kept living my life over repeatedly in my mind, I could somehow change it, make it better. But no matter how I thought it up, it ended the same. My life had no purpose, and I didn't know who I was. Inside my mind, my father was still beating me up, belittling me, and criticizing me.

I faded so deep into the darkness during this time that even I became afraid. Would I have the strength to get out? Sometimes it was like watching someone else, someone who was not me at all. The inward me seemed to be in control while the outward me was rapidly beginning to lose control.

I was seeing Dr. Klein during this time as often as I could, but even that was a farce. I would get in his office and not be able to tell him what was going on. I gave him such a small bit of information that it was a wonder he could figure out what was going on with me. He told me that he was concerned about me. Just his saying he was concerned did a lot for me. It was like there was one person in the world who knew I was having a problem, and he cared enough to be concerned. I was such a fake. I could pull off "everything is great" in front of most the world and get away with it. At least I thought I could.

I did have a problem at work for a while during this time. It was clear I was not keeping myself up as good as was customary for me. My desk was in a place that was visible to everyone, and I began to feel like I was on display. I just knew everyone was looking at me, and I felt like I was baring all, and that terrified me. I wanted to hide under the desk, but that would be too obvious. When my boss's office was empty one day, I went in there and closed the door partway so I could see out by leaning forward from the chair, but by leaning back just a little, no one could see me there.

When my boss finally came back to his office, I told him I needed to go home. I left, and he called my stepbrother and told him I needed some help. John came over. My main concern was what to do with Darchele since, at this point, I wasn't sure what course this was going to take. John told me to call Dr. Klein, which I did while he was there. He agreed to see me the next day. John agreed to take Darchele for the evening but no more. While he was there, a friend of mine who lived upstairs dropped in, and John suggested we go out to dinner and maybe to the spa. He gave me some money for the evening's expenses and said I should not sit in the apartment all by myself all evening.

Pattie and I went out to dinner, and it was the first decent food I'd had in a week. Then we went to the spa. The thing I remember most about that evening was the steam room. I could have stayed there for a year. There was something very comforting about the heat and steam. I felt like I was cradled in some big warm arms, and I felt so safe at that moment, I just knew everything was going to be okay. It was as if I had hit bottom and was bouncing back up. At least it was a start. The next thing I needed to do was get some sleep, something I'd had very little of the past week.

The next day was better after talking with Dr. Klein. I finally found the courage to share with him things I'd been keeping secret for years. He told me that the things abused children do and the choices they make as children are not surprising or shocking. That made me feel a bit better; at least he was not shocked and horrified.

I missed the next day of work. When I went in the following day, I talked to my boss and got things straightened out there.

I started power walking ten miles a day, and that helped. Darchele would ride her bike with me sometimes. She thought that was great fun. I did two and a half miles four times a day. I was still working on my relationship with Darchele and desperately trying to make it better.

One weekend Darrow's parents picked up Darchele to stay with them for the weekend. They knew Darchele was not to be alone with Darrow, and I trusted them. His mother knew I loved him, and that the divorce was necessary. She understood that.

When they brought her home, Darchele could hardly wait for them to leave. When the door shut, she told me that her dad took her to lunch. After that, on the way home in the car he put his hand between her legs and asked her if she'd like to go over to his place, so they could take off their clothes and play a while. She hit him and said, "No!" Thank God he did not push it and took her back to her grandparents' house. I was so angry that they had let her go to lunch alone with him.

I waited until her grandparents had time to get home and I called. I told her grandmother that I couldn't trust her with Darchele anymore. She said Darrow had been so good she didn't think him taking her to lunch would be a problem. I explained what Darchele had told me, and she was shocked and so sorry. I told her in the future that they would have to visit her at our place, or I'd bring her to their house and stay with her. She didn't see her grandparents much after that. Her choice.

Her father would call occasionally, but she always ended up in tears. I told her she didn't have to talk to him if she didn't want to.

Then I met Paula, Dr. Klein's receptionist, and all hell broke loose.

Paula the Sneak

June 1984

Oh My God,
How could I get into something like this? From the frying pan into the fire. I thought we were friends. She was such a sneak. She lied to me and took advantage of me. As usual, I believed all her lies. Why do I believe everything everyone says? How stupid. I need to use my head; there were clues, and I ignored them. Now I'm paying the price.

Poor Darchele, she thinks we are all friends and doesn't understand what is happening. I feel so bad for her. Why isn't there something in this universe that protects children from their parents' mistakes?

Two moves in less than three months; that's even a bit much for me.

What next?

Michele

I can't believe I let myself into this situation. I guess one would say I was vulnerable. I met Paula at my psychiatrist's office. She was the receptionist. Who would've ever dreamed that the receptionist in a psychiatrist office would be anything other than a nice, well-adjusted person?

I would get to my appointment with Dr. Klein early, and she and I enjoyed talking. At that time, my weight was way down, and I was still speed walking about ten miles a day and doing regular exercises as well. Paula was into physical fitness, and we would talk about that as well as other things. The relationship grew, and one day, we planned to meet for a drink after my session, which was about the same time she got off work.

We were the same age, which was nice. Paula was married but had no children, although she liked children. The night we met after she got off work, we had quite a chat. She was having problems with her husband and was planning to leave him. By the time the conversation was over, we had decided to move in together. She couldn't afford to live on her own, and I really liked her. I thought if Darchele liked her that it would be a nice situation.

I had just planned a trip to Boston to visit my dad and his third wife, Joanne. God knows why I would keep putting myself through that; he never changed, although I liked Joanne. Darchele was still in Arkansas for the summer with my mother and Bill. We had a cat, and Paula offered to stay in our apartment while I was gone. Darchele got home in a couple of weeks, and Paula came over one day to meet her. Darchele liked her, so it was settled.

I invited Paula to come to a family gathering on the fourth of July at my stepbrother's. Everyone seemed to like her. It wasn't until our relationship was over that people told me there was something about her they didn't like, but they couldn't put their finger on it.

We checked the apartments where I was living for a vacancy of a three-bedroom apartment, which they had, and we rented it. We had three weeks before the move. I went out and bought us a washer and dryer since the place we were moving into was a townhouse with a basement. It was going to be great to be able to do laundry at home. This was an exciting time. Even though I had the feeling things had moved too fast, I kept pushing all doubts aside.

I was shopping with Paula one evening when she got angry with the salesclerk. I felt she was unreasonable. I said nothing, but it bothered me. At my next appointment with Dr. Klein, I mentioned I was having some second thoughts about the girl I was planning on living with. I figured it was probably nothing more than "pre-marital jitters" so to speak, and I don't recall him saying much about it.

Paula had asked me not to tell them at the clinic that she and I saw each other socially, and of course, that meant not to say anything about us moving in together, for sure. I had not told Dr. Klein who my new roommate was. I sometimes wonder if he had any thoughts about the fact that I never gave my friend a name.

Paula asked me next time I saw her if I was having second thoughts about moving in with her, and it occurred to me that she knew about my last session with Dr. Klein. I told her I was just a little nervous.

Then I asked her right out, "Do you mean to tell me you read what Dr. Klein writes about our sessions?"

"Yes, do you want to know what else he said?"

"No, I don't think I do."

I was curious, but I was suddenly feeling very uncomfortable. My sessions with Dr. Klein were no longer private. They were now between three people. I had told Paula a lot about myself, and I thought she had told me a lot about herself, but she had told me nothing until the day of our move.

That was quite a day. Paula was not a very good packer and most of her boxes didn't even have tops on them. The movers were late as usual, but finally picked up her things and then stopped at my place and loaded my items. They weren't very professional, but they were cheap, and I guess you get what you pay for. They said they knew how to move a piano, but my piano ended up in the middle of my living room floor upside down. I couldn't watch anymore and left the apartment. It is a miracle the piano survived the move, but it did.

After everything was in the new place, we decided it was time for some lunch. We went over to the restaurant around the corner and ran into Bev, another friend of mine from the bank.

She joined us for lunch. Sometime during lunch, it came out that Paula had spent ten years in a mental hospital. *Ten years.* I was shocked but didn't let on right then that it bothered me. For her to get employment, friends and relatives had let her use them as work references to cover the last ten years. She explained that she was a depressed young woman and her parents had her put in the hospital, but she felt it wasn't necessary. I couldn't believe that a mistake could go undetected for *ten years*. I sympathized with her about how awful it must have been.

How could I get into the same situation twice? I walked into it with Darchele's dad with my eyes wide open, but this was different. How could she have done this to me? That was a secret she had no right to keep from someone she planned to live with, especially someone who just came from a marriage with a man who spent a good deal of his time in a mental hospital. She owed it to herself, as well as me, to see if I was going to react before we moved in together. Not telling me about this was very wrong.

We went back to the apartment and unpacked things and started to settle in. That evening we got on the subject of jewelry, and I went to show Paula a piece of mine. I discovered it was missing, along with several other items. One of the movers had taken some of my jewelry. Well, a perfect ending to a perfect day.

I contacted the police the next day, and after a few days, a detective had recovered one of my rings. He asked if I wanted to press charges. Before I answered, he explained that I probably wouldn't get any satisfaction. The young man lived in a one-room apartment with his pregnant wife and another small child. He said he shook the kid up and hoped it would be enough to make him think before he ever tried it again. I didn't press charges, and in no time, the whole incident was forgotten. I had other things to cope with.

Paula and I lived together for less than three months. That is all the time it took to almost destroy both of us.

I tried to tell her once how I felt about what she had done, but all I could do was cry. I was angry at her about the way she told me. At the time, I didn't want to hurt her by telling her she was wrong, and that I didn't trust her anymore, especially when I thought back to about how angry she got with that salesclerk. I had always been afraid of anger in other people. Although telling her wouldn't have changed what ultimately happened, I am sure she knew what she had done.

In a short time, I found these were important issues I needed to discuss with Dr. Klein, but I couldn't even hint at them because it involved Paula. I told him one day that, for reasons I couldn't tell him, I had to stop seeing him. He didn't pry, but wished me well and said goodbye.

I told Paula that night I would not see Dr. Klein anymore because I didn't feel right lying to him about our situation. Paula was nice about it and said she didn't want me to stop seeing him because of her; she knew how much I liked him. She said if I felt I had to tell him to go ahead, but she wished I wouldn't. That was all I needed to hear. I called Dr. Klein from work the next day and asked to see him again. I told him that the situation had changed, and I had something I needed to tell him.

I went in that evening and told him about Paula and me, but not about her reading the reports and not about her stay in the hospital. We were still living together, and at the time, I still hoped we could save the relationship. I should have known better; a relationship built on dishonesty will never last.

I was surprised at Dr. Klein's reaction. He was very angry with Paula. I said it was as much my fault as hers, but he disagreed. He said she was interfering with a therapist and his patient. I was vulnerable, and she took advantage of me. I didn't think of it then, but he knew she was typing up his notes from my sessions, so he knew how wrong this was.

The next day when she went to work, she expected something to be said, but never expected what she got. Dr. Klein called her into his office and shouted at her. He said she had acted unprofessionally and what she did was grounds for dismissal, and he would take it before the board and recommend that be done. WOW! I never expected she would be fired, but I should have.

It didn't happen right away, since other members of the clinic liked her and fought his action. However, it did eventually happen. I had to stop seeing Dr. Klein anyway because I could not trust Paula not to read my reports. What had I gained by telling? Nothing!

Everything went wrong from that point on. Paula picked at everything I did or didn't do. She got upset because I put the hairbrush down on the counter in the bathroom too hard when I was getting ready for work in the morning, and she could hear it in her room. If I didn't wipe Darchele's fingerprints off everything every day, it annoyed her. I suddenly became afraid of her anger. I couldn't be honest with her about my feelings. Everything I felt led back to the fact she had been in some mental hospital for ten years, and never told me until the day we moved in together. I couldn't seem to get past that. I didn't trust her anymore. What else was she not telling me?

I started planning to move. I had as much packed as I could and still live there. Paula knew I was leaving, but that was not enough. I told her I would be sure she had a month's notice to make whatever arrangements she needed to make. She insisted on knowing right then the day I was leaving. I told her we would be out on the first of December, even if I had to put my things in storage and move into a motel with Darchele until we could find a place. We never spoke again. She was rude and nasty to Darchele, who was in the third grade at that time. This hurt her a lot because she thought we were all friends and didn't understand how this could happen.

I scheduled the movers to come, but I still didn't have a place to rent and began to think we may have to stay in a motel. The day before the movers came, I found and rented a place.

I finally did go back and see Dr. Klein for another year and told him the whole story about Paula, including her ten years stay in the mental hospital and about her family giving her work references for her resume for that time. I also told him about her reading my records, which I was sure he already knew. He was as shocked as I was when he heard about her stay in the hospital. When he told the others on the board, she was immediately fired.

Of course, they changed the procedures at the clinic to prevent the receptionist from typing the reports for the clients they saw in the office. They had another clinic and sent the reports back and forth between them for typing. No one saw the reports for the people they were greeting in the office.

I sometimes feel our breakup was my fault because of my reaction to what she told me about her hospital stay, and my inability to discuss it with her openly and honestly. Then I think that no, she was wrong about not telling me before we moved in together, and for reading my session reports. She took advantage of me.

Once again, I ran from another unpleasant situation. I didn't deal with it; I hid from it. Why was I so afraid to speak up for myself?

I rented a condominium, and Darchele and I moved once again, and that was another nightmare.

In the Darkness

Dec. 5, 1983 1:00 am

Dear Dr. Klein,
 I've sure made a shamble of everything, and now I'm so depressed I can't seem to get motivated to do anything, except what's necessary to keep me alive: work, eat, and sleep. My apartment is a mess. I've unpacked only what was necessary and left boxes stacked everywhere. The things sitting around depress me even more, but I just look at them and cry, instead of getting up and unpacking and making this place home. Poor Darchele; Christmas is coming, and again I do nothing. I can sit around and wish this, that, and the other thing, but what's happened has happened, and I can't wish it gone.
 I feel myself retreating even more from the rest of the human race. I need them, and I want them, but I can't seem to get away from them fast enough. I'm afraid every time I walk out my door that one of my neighbors might be standing there. God, I don't want to go back to that dark place, but that's where I'm heading. I worked so hard to get out, where did all

the fight go? Why, why, why do I just sit and let myself slide back and do nothing? I wish I could see you every day. I can't seem to stop crying.

Talk about a poor self-image. I've got a whopper. I'm such an ass.

I find myself wondering, what's life all about? What purpose does it serve? Why are we here? Where are we going? What is happiness? Does anyone have it? Happiness comes from within. We make our own misery. Laugh and the world laughs with you, cry, and you cry alone.

I don't want to be alone. I don't want to cry. God, please help me to see the light. Make me understand. Where is this happiness that's inside? How do I find it? I know, I know, I'm the only one that can find my happiness. I WILL FIND IT. I won't give up. I refuse to give up.

I know what my biggest problem is: I won't speak up. But why? Why? What am I so damned afraid of? Experience the feeling, that's what you said. Is that it? Am I afraid of what I'll feel if I speak up for myself? God, could it possibly be any worse than the way I feel because I don't speak up? NO. Now if that is true and I know that, then why don't I be kind to myself and open my big mouth?

Damn, am I ever angry. Why? Because I feel Paula did a job on me. I did one on her too, so I guess we're even. Two wrongs don't make a right.

I'll be, I'm starting to feel better. Could it be that I wrote myself out of my depression? I even think maybe tomorrow I'll do some unpacking; it's too late tonight. I read somewhere that if you're feeling down, if you write, sometimes it helps. There must be something to it because I do feel better.

I do want to thank you for your time. You've been quite a help.

See you next week, same time, same place.
As ever, Michele

In the months that we lived in the condo, I was still seeing Dr. Klein, but I couldn't tell him what I was thinking. I was so afraid of someone knowing how messed up I was.

I started writing him letters that were never mailed. It was kind of like a journal for the months that we lived in the condominium. I wrote to him everything that was going through my mind, and how I actually felt. I think this was probably the lowest point of my life.

I kept these letters in a lock box for many years, along with other notes I made about what was going on in my life. I am glad I did, because they helped when writing this book.

The following are some of the letters I wrote. They show how confused and mixed up I was. If I had told the doctor, maybe it would not have taken so long to get through it. I was a bit embarrassed about how these letters made me look and was tempted not to include them but decided they were part of the process and needed to be seen.

I was pretty bummed out when we moved into our new place and couldn't even unpack. I just took out what we needed and left the rest. Every night I would sit there looking at the floor, going over and over in my head what had happened. What was wrong with me, why did I keep getting into these weird relationships?

Dec 5, 1983 10:00 am

Hi Doc,

It's me again. Gee last night I was feeling pretty good, and I got up this morning feeling really down again. Now nothing happened between last night and this morning, so why did my mood change? I guess nothing was solved last night; I just wrote myself into a little high, and by morning, it was gone. Suppose I can do it again? Well, it's worth a try.

Between my job being so busy I can hardly stand the pressure, and my home life needs a lot of strength, which I don't have, I'm really in a bind. I feel physically weak and mentally drained. I need rest, and I can't see any insight. I must say I'm a bit concerned about my health, physical as well as mental. I don't eat right, and I don't think right. I get dizzy and my head pounds, my stomach is upset, and I could cry all day. I control it, but my control is growing weaker all the time.

I'm tired of pretending all day at work that everything is fine when things are not well at all. I keep telling myself to hang in there, things will get better, but they don't. I have four days of work sitting on my desk and no sign of it letting up.

Michele

Dec. 6, 1983

Hi Doc,

Well, I guess it just took some time to wear off. I feel fine now. The tears seem to have dried up, and I'm on my way again. I got a lot of unpacking done today. It seems I'm finding that the sky doesn't fall in when things aren't done right on schedule. I think I may even start to like this place if I try.

The day after tomorrow is Thursday again, and I made it another week. Although I had my doubts at first, all's well, that ends well.

I look forward to seeing you each week. I don't know if that's good or bad, but I do. You know, I think writing has helped.

Michele

Dec. 10, 1983

Hi Doc,

It's me again. Boy, what a day. I can't believe the anger that's starting to spill out of me, and the bad language I'm using. Words I've never used before. Temper tantrums like a three-year-old. I worry that I might lose control somewhere out in public or say something I'll regret. I've come close a few times. I can't believe how self-centered it all is. Look out world, here I come, and I pity the people who get in my way. As if I'm the only one in the world with places to go and things to do. I've been taking some tranquilizers, but I don't want to get hung up on them. They seem to help some, but I'd rather cure the problem than treat the symptoms. But while I'm trying to get the cure, I can't go around hurting the people I care about.

I really should be getting Darchele some help too, but I can't afford both of us. So again, she gets sacrificed. What an injustice I've done to her. I should *have remained childless. It's not her fault her mother's so screwed up, but just the same, she suffers for it. I may not beat her physically, but I pound the hell out of her mentally, and that's just as bad, maybe worse. I wish there were pills I could take that would make me instant wonderful Mother.*

Now on top of everything else, I have to learn to control an ever-mounting temper and stop the swearing.

It's time for bed. Thanks again for your time. As always, you're quite helpful. Looking forward to seeing you Thursday.

As always, Michele

Dec. 18, 1983

Hi Doc,

Things seem to be going better now. I think this place I'm living in is almost a place to call home. I'm even starting to like it.

Darchele's still a little unhappy. I wish I could make her happier, but I guess, like me, she must decide for herself she wants to be happy before it can happen. I hopefully can guide her a little, but I can't make her happy.

Michele

Feb. 12, 1984

Hi Doc,

Boy, what a day. It started great then the bottom fell out. I'm gaining weight. I've completely lost control of my eating and spending.

Michele

March 27, 1984

Hi Doc,

It's been about ten weeks since we last met. Up until about six weeks ago, everything seemed to be going fine. Then it happened. I met a man. A man I wanted to see again and again, and lucky me, he felt the same. Or was I lucky? I'm scared to death, full of doubt, and I'm not sure what to do. I keep telling myself one day at a time, but that doesn't seem to help, the fear is still there. I find myself near tears a lot again and impatient with Darchele.

Michele

OUT OF DARKNESS, INTO THE LIGHT

March 30, 1984

Hi Doc,

It's me again, I've had a few drinks, and so you'll have to forgive me. My whole life seems to be taking a turn. I'm not sure if it's good or bad, but it's turning. Gary seems to bring out the worst and the best in me.

The Thursday depression was bad this week. I'm not sure I understand it. I believe I know where it comes from, but why I'm not sure. I think I'm going to call you on Monday. I've got to figure this out, so I can get on with this relationship and skip the Thursday depression.

I think I like Gary, but I need more time to be sure. I need to see him under more circumstances, and with other people around. I only know him alone, and I need more to see if I can get along with him in different phases of life.

I look forward to seeing him, but why? I've got to stop asking that. One day at a time. One day at a time. I try, but it's so hard.

I like him, but why? Is it because he likes me, or because I like him? Damn. Do I or don't I want to get involved. Yes and No. Wish I could make up my mind.

I like having a few drinks before he comes, but it worries me. I sure hope I don't have alcoholic tendencies. NO NOT ME. I bet that's what they all say, HA! HA!

Oh, Gary, hurry up. I hate waiting. I long to feel you close to me. Oh, such a feeling to have a man close. It's not the sex, just the closeness. Touch me. Hold me. I can live without it, but I don't want to.
As Ever, your Patient,
Michele

When I met Gary, it gave me some incentive to finish unpacking and decorate our new place. He worked an odd shift, so during the week, we could only get together late at night. He would show up at midnight or later. On the weekends, we saw each other during the day. It took a while, but Darchele finally accepted him. For that, I am sorry.

I finally figured out that he was only using me for sex. I gathered up the few things he had left at my place and sent him packing. Gary was the last person I ever dated.

August 9, 1984

Hi Doc,
Hope you don't mind if I refer to you that way. I've been writing you letters for over a year now, and

that's the way I started them all. Just because I'm seriously considering mailing this one, is no reason to start it differently.

When I left your office today, I was upset because I didn't say the things I intended to say. I could write what I wanted to say, and that would be a start. I feel a little silly doing this, but here goes.

The person that lives inside my head is totally different than the person on the surface. Occasionally, that person gets a little closer to the surface, and it scares me. I think that's who I'm hiding from. She's not right, and I don't like her. I'm afraid of losing control.

Sometimes I get angry with you, but it's not your fault. I hate waiting till Thursday when sometimes I want to talk on Monday or Tuesday. But who knows, if I saw you one of those times maybe I wouldn't talk then either.

This is a laugh; I see you because I need help with the way I handle things, and then when I need you the most I don't talk because I'm afraid you'll think something's wrong with me. That's funny.

I guess what's more important than that person inside, is why I keep allowing her to come back. What starts it? It's like what comes first, the chicken or the egg? Do I do things I don't think are right causing her to come up, or does she come around and cause me to go on a binge?

I should go to bed, but I don't want to. That's not good, and I know it, but still, here I sit. Why do I do things I know I shouldn't?

I want to talk to you now. I don't know how to start a relationship. I'm not bad at finishing them. I can talk about things after they happen, but not while they're going on. I can tell you what I thought a minute ago but not what I'm thinking now. Does that even make sense?

It would be so easy just to let myself go. Then someone else would take care of me. I wouldn't have to think about anything. I can't do that; I have to take care of Darchele. God knew what he was doing when he let me have her. She's my salvation.

I'm so angry, hostile, and bitter, I can hardly believe it. I didn't think I was capable of this kind of reaction.

Michele

I chickened out and never sent the above letter.

Sept. 6, 1984

Hi Doc,

Today's visit has me going. What we were saying about my dad. I think its anger I feel, but not sure.

Why, why did he do it? Damn him. What did he think he was doing? I wonder if he's pleased with what he created. I wonder if he's happy now. Damn him. I can't make him go away, but I can make me go away.
Michele

Sept. 7, 1984

Hi Doc,

Seeing you is like an equalizer; it helps me make it from one week to the next, and to miss one week seems like forever. God, I wish I could open up to you easier. It's like everything is a big secret. I'm afraid to let even you know what's inside me. It comes, but so slow. There's so much I want to say. I need to trust someone completely. I trust you more than anyone, but even you not completely. It's getting there, but it's taken over five years to get there. What's real? Sometimes I can't seem to tell what's in my head and what's real. It's getting all mixed up.

Right now, I'm confused, caught between fighting and giving up. Sometimes I wish I could see you every day. I want to ask you what to do, but I know you'll only turn it around and ask me what I think I should do. The corner of that room is so warm and inviting sometimes. It would be so easy to curl up in a corner and turn off completely.

It's so easy to say I am important, what I want is important, but I feel nothing. It's those two people again. One saying get the world it's yours, the other saying you're nothing, nothing, nothing. Take the crumbs, that's all you're worth. But I am worth more. I have rights, just like everyone.

Damn him, what right did he have to train me like a dog: obey commands, follow instructions, don't feel, just act; what right did he have? I wish I could hate him, but I can't anymore. I wish I could hurt him, but I can't. I wish I could disappear.

OH GOD, I WISH YOU WERE HERE, DOC.

Michele

Hi Doc,

I made it through the weekend. I didn't think I would on Friday but here it is Monday, and all is well. It's funny how awful things can seem one day, and I wake up the next day on top of the world. I felt good yesterday, energetic, active, and up. I even felt good this morning. I don't understand what's going on. One day my mind is full of insanity and confusion, and the next I'm fine. Why?

OUT OF DARKNESS, INTO THE LIGHT

I'm composing a letter in my head to my father and going to tell him in the nicest way possible to get out of my life.

Michele

This next letter I wrote to my dad, telling him as nice as I could that I didn't want anything from him, and for him to stay out of my life. I did not mail it.

Sept. 10, 1984

Dear Dad,

I appreciate what you've offered to do for me, but I'm not ready to accept your offer. I don't want to feel I owe you anything. Plus, your offer seemed odd and had strings attached. I don't want to see you. Do you think you can make up for the fact that you were an unfeeling, brutal father when I was a child? I'm sorry, but I haven't forgiven you yet, and I don't want your help. Where was your help when I needed it while I was growing up? You didn't raise me, you trained me like a dog, but you missed something; even a dog needs love. Where was your love when I was growing up? I don't want it now. It's too late. You had your chance. I don't understand what you thought you were doing. You've screwed up my thinking so much; I don't know if I'll ever be straight again.

Michele

Sept. 10, 1984

Hi Doc,

Ten more days seems like such a long time. I'm ready to talk now. I want to get it all out and understand it, so I can turn things around and stop all this bizarre thinking.

I feel rather sad tonight. As usual, I'm not sure why.

Can you tell me why I seem to be getting worse instead of better? My thinking seems to be far worse now than it's ever been before.

I never used to ask myself why things happened. They just did, and I went from there.

Sometimes I think of doing things deliberately to set myself off. Why? That's so self-destructive. I know I must get enough sleep, or I get down. I'll look at the clock some nights and it's time I should go to bed, but I don't want to. I want to stay up, I don't want to sleep. But why? I just sit there and think.

All the talking and thinking in the world won't change a thing unless I'm willing to start taking risks. I'm not sure I can. I'm still so full of fear.

I'm even afraid of being afraid. Fear is your own worst enemy. The things you fear the most always come to you. I'm afraid of being crazy. But at the same time, there's something very inviting about it. But I couldn't do that to Darchele. Her father is already past the point of no return. Maybe that's why God decided to let me have a child. A reason for me to fight. How could he take a chance like that? What if I don't make it? Poor Darchele, it isn't fair. But then what in life is fair?

I'll never slip over the edge because there's one thing I fear more than anything else; not being able to take care of Darchele and myself, pay my bills, etc. If I couldn't work, it'd be over.

Time to go to bed like a good girl.

Good night, as ever

Michele

Sept. 11, 1984 11:30am

Hi Doc,

I bet if you ever read these letters you'd think I was weird.

I get upset with myself when I don't talk in your office. I mean really, I only get forty-five minutes a week, and you'd think I'd make the best use of it. I can hear you saying, "Why don't you talk, what do you think will happen if you speak up?"

Maybe I'm afraid of change. I keep thinking I won't be me anymore. I'll turn into someone I don't even know. That's a laugh. I don't like who I am, so what could be so awful about being different? After all, isn't that why I came to you in the first place?

You know, sometimes I like myself, why does that part of me only peek out on occasion?

Why have I divided myself into sections?

There's the part I like:

Witty, charming, intelligent, humorous, compassionate, feeling, understanding, ambitious, and a good mother.

There's the part I don't like:

Quiet, fearful, forgetful, irritable, self-centered, angry, inactive, and a bad mother. Too into myself to see anyone else's needs.

There's the part I'm afraid of:

Crazy, irrational, unreasonable, wants to be alone. Hiding, wanting to run away. Wanting to die.

I'm sure there's more. I never seem to know which me is going to be there when I get up, or if it will be the same when I go to bed. I'm sure something triggers them off, but what? What little-unnoticed thing causes the change in me, and why?

As ever, Michele

OUT OF DARKNESS, INTO THE LIGHT

September 11, 1984 6:30pm

Hi Doc,

Gee this is getting to be a habit. While fixing dinner, I'm thinking about writing to you. I wish I had asked you for another appointment, so I didn't have to skip a week. Although right now I feel quite comfortable with missing a week. I'm feeling quite relaxed right now. Now that's weird, just as I write this I can feel myself slipping down. A sudden feeling of tears about to spill over. Now, what happened? I wish someone were here. I like to have company. I'm starting to like Nancy a lot, but like all my relationships, I wonder how long it will last. Nancy will last a while; she and I seem to have some things in common.

I was thinking it might be nice to have a man around sometimes for Darchele. But it can't be just anyone. I must be able to like him and trust him with Darchele. That's as hard to find as a serious boyfriend.

A coworker is bringing her typewriter to work for me tomorrow. I'm going to get started on retyping my resume. That's step one at finding a new job. If I'm going to be single the rest of my life I need a better job and more money. I think I'm ready now to get started on getting my life in order. Guess it's about time.

I've got to stop now; I have other things to do. It's been great talking to you.
As Ever, Michele

Sept. 12, 1984 10:45pm

Hi Doc,

Boy, what a mess I'm in with this place I'm living in. I have a cold, I don't feel well, and everything seems to be going wrong.

I thought I had time, but it seems I don't. The new owners want me out. I am so upset. I'm taking Thursday and Friday off work to see if I can find a place to live. Why me, is this some kind of test? Is someone trying to see how far they can push me before I break? Well, I won't do it. I must hold up and I will. But damn it, right now I feel like breaking down, but I know it's because I don't feel well. I'm going to bed.
More another time.
Michele

"...from the frying pan into the fire." A woman who moved to California owned the place I rented. While I lived there, the condominium went into foreclosure, there was a big battle over who owned the place, and I was right in the middle of it. I had two people wanting my rent payment, and a realtor calling all the time wanting to show the place. I finally stopped answering the phone.

I stopped giving anyone my rent payment and just set it aside until I saw some legal documents of ownership, which never happened. Someone from the condominium management office called about past due association fees. Since they were not paid, I couldn't use the laundry facilities or the pool.

Sept. 13, 1984 5:30pm

Hi Doc,

I am so down today. What makes it worse is I still feel physically bad, and don't have the energy to attack the problem the way I should. It's raining, and that doesn't help. I feel beaten. I have nowhere to turn anymore. I give up, but I can't, I must do something, or my things will be moved out into the street when my time is up. God, why me? The fight is gone; let the world do what it wants with me. I can't do anything else. I quit; leave me alone world. Corner, here I come. Darchele, you poor child. None of this is your fault, yet you pay the price. I hate this life. I wish I were dead.

Michele

Sept. 15, 1984

Hi Doc,

I guess all's well that ends well. I have a new place to live. We're moving in five days. Darchele's excited, and that pleases me.

Michele

Sept. 16, 1984 9:10pm

Hi Doc,

Well, it's been a busy day, and I just put Darchele to bed, and I suddenly feel let down. I have about half of my packing done. I have big plans for the new place. I'm unpacking everything and what I don't use or have room for, I'm getting rid of it. I'm staying in this place for a long time. No more moves. Once I get settled in and relaxed, I'm starting to look for a new job. This time I'm really going to do it. I'm also cutting my dad out.

Writing spree is over. After this, no more till after I move.

Are you going to be surprised Thursday. So much has happened.

Michele

Sept. 17, 1984 10:05pm

Hi Doc,

Just stopped packing for tonight and thought I'd drop you a few lines.

Too much is happening too fast. What I want to do is sit down and cry.

Now I have a possible job opportunity. The thought of doing final moving preparations and going on a job interview, all in one day, and then moving the next morning seems like so much. During this time, I also must get Darchele enrolled in school. God, will I ever get everything done? Of course, I have no choice but to do it. I will get it done, and everything will turn out fine, but my insides are going to be a mess in the process.

Why does this job opportunity scare me so much? Just as I wrote that something came over me. It's all going to be okay. This job isn't life or death. If I get it great, if I don't, a better one will come along. I need to relax. Get to the interview twenty minutes early and meditate in the car for a while.

God, I missed you last week. It's been a long time.
Love, Michele

I finally found another place and moved out without telling anyone. I took the money I had set aside and used it for the first and last months' rent in the new place. I never heard from anyone there after that. We lived in the condominium for one school year for Darchele.

The idea of this new place makes me feel hopeful.

Finding the Light

June 1985

Hello God,

WOW, are you really there? Sorry, it has taken me so long to find you. This is not going to be easy. I am still not sure about you, but I'm getting a feeling that maybe you can help me. I am still finding my way out of the darkness, but I'm starting to see a bit of light. I read in II Timothy 1:7, "God hath not given us the spirit of fear; but of power, and of love, and of a sound mind." I think I might have found something that will help me to experience that in my life, to live without fear, to have a sound mind and be able to love.

I am learning that it's not someone to love me that I am seeking. I need to be able to give love without hesitation, fully and completely. I thought I'd found that with Darrow, but when I think about it now, even that was not true love. True love is giving myself totally, without a doubt over to God; to trust him completely.

I don't know if I can do that. To trust something I cannot experience with the five physical senses: feel, hear, touch, taste, smell. I want freedom from this hell I've been living in for the last forty-two years, and nothing else has worked, so this is worth a try.

God, please be patient with me. I am new at this.

Michele

Our new place was perfect. It had everything to make both Darchele and me happy. It was a duplex with a small yard. I knew the minute we moved in this was home. Our lives started to take shape. We got a puppy, Babe, so Darchele would have someone there when she got home from school and wouldn't be alone. She was thrilled. We had tried a couple of cats in other places, but they did not work out. She just was not a cat person.

I had attended Sunday school for about ten years when I was growing up, although what I was being taught was not practiced at home. My father had taken us, and that was a real ordeal. He would sit us down Sunday morning and drill us on that week's Sunday school lesson so we would not embarrass him. Can you believe he taught Sunday school? Thank God, not my class. I couldn't get into the Bible thing and left as soon as I was old enough to stop going. I did learn some things, so it was not a total waste.

On Sunday, I was taught love and forgiveness, and was then abused the rest of the week. When I was sixteen, based on the actions of one man, I decided if this was religion, who needed it. It wasn't until much later that I learned that you couldn't judge any religion by the people who attend the church; you must study their religious doctrine or tenets or whatever books were published by the founder of that religion for yourself, and not judge it based on the attendees.

For years, a religious textbook sat on my bookshelf and collected dust. Then one day, someone gave me a book about the discoverer and founder of that religion. I picked it up several times and started to read it. I hadn't gotten into it too far when a friend asked me a question regarding that religion. I didn't know the answer, but something told me the answer was in the textbook.

Curious about the answer, I dusted off the book and started thumbing through it. I tried to find the answer on a hit-and-miss basis, without much luck, so I opened it to the first page and started reading. I became so engrossed I couldn't put it down. After a while, something would tell me to shift gears and read some more of the founder's *Years of Discovery*, which I soon finished. The book was part of a trilogy, and I was eager to know more about this woman, so I purchased the *Years of Trial and the Years of Authority*. I spent every minute of my spare time for the next month or so reading the textbook and the trilogy.

I started learning things that would make my life better and make me a better mother. I learned that I was the one who was messing up my life. I had to take responsibility for my actions and stop blaming everyone and everything else.

I started attending church, and my bank friends laughed and said that going to church was just another self-help binge, and that I would quit after a while. For several years, I had been reading self-help books. Always jumping from one thing to another, and nothing seemed to help, I still felt the same. My life had no purpose. Why was I here?

With what I was learning now, I knew I'd found the "pearl of great price." I was so excited about what I was reading that I couldn't stop talking about it. It didn't take long to realize the people I knew at the time didn't have the vaguest idea of what I was talking about, so I started keeping this newfound joy to myself.

For twenty-five years, I couldn't even say the word God. If I referred to a supreme power of some kind, I called it Joe. I wasn't sure how to define "God." I couldn't conceive of a power out there, that created man and the universe, and that it was all good. It didn't make sense. If that was true, why was my life such a mess, certainly anything but good.

One passage in the Bible got me thinking. It is from Genesis 1: 26-28

26 And God said, Let us make man in our image, after our likeness: and let them have dominion over the fish of the sea, and over the fowl of the air, and over the cattle, and over all the earth, and over every creeping thing that creepeth upon the earth.

27 So God created man in his own image, in the image of God created he him; male and female created he them.

28 And God blessed them, and God said unto them, be fruitful, and multiply, and replenish the earth, and subdue it: and have dominion over the fish of the sea, and over the fowl of the air, and over every living thing that moveth upon the earth.

In verse 26, the writer states, "let *us* make man in *our* image"—*our* image. That said to me that there are two aspects to God; he is both Father and Mother, both protector and nurturer.

He also writes, "let them have dominion..." WOW; God has dominion over all his/her creation. That was not surprising, but that we, as his image and likeness, also have dominion over all that he created was something I would have to think about. To me, that meant I had control over my life. Not over what went on around me, but over how I reacted to those things; that was my responsibility.

I was learning how to define God. God loved all his creation, which included me, and I wasn't an awful, unlovable person. We may make mistakes in our lives, but He didn't make mistakes when he created His children. "He saw everything that he had made and behold it was very good." This included me. I was starting to understand what that meant. God is Love, Spirit, Principle, and much more. If I could think of Him that way, rather than some holy being ruling over his people, it made more sense to me.

The dictionary defines principle in many ways. Here are some of them that apply in my mind to God.

Principle: "The main form of the verb, which expresses existence, from which all other forms are derived." This means to me that the main form of existence is God as Creator, he is a state of being, and we are derived from him. We have his DNA and all things good. Anything that is not good does not come from God. It doesn't matter who our human parents are, we are his children, and my divine Father/Mother loves me unconditionally.

"Principle is a fundamental truth for a chain of reasoning." Everything should be reasoned from God (cause) to his creation (effect) man, and the universe. A priori reasoning is correct reasoning, cause to effect. Reasoning from an effect back to cause is ambiguous, and never accomplishes anything; it is backward.

"Principle is a basic source, a Law, a fixed rule of conduct." God is our source, and that source is Love, He is the law of Love, and the fixed rule of conduct is Love. I had to learn to love myself as his child. I was learning that I didn't have to look back to see who I was; I only had to look at right now. I am a good person right now.

There's a story in the Bible about an immoral woman caught in the act. In St. John 8: 3-11, Jesus said, "He that is without sin among you, let him first cast a stone at her." They all saw that they were not sinless and left, and Jesus said to the woman, "go and sin no more." That tells me when I stop sinning, I am forgiven. That punishment for my sins stops when I stop sinning, and there would be no judgment for my past sins.

I knew right then that my sins of immorality were forgiven because I had stopped sinning. My life started to change, but that didn't happen overnight. It took one step at a time. I was beginning to turn from the darkness to the light.

I remember reading in Matthew 6:6, "But thou, when thou prayest, enter into thy closet, and when thou hast shut thy door, pray to thy Father which is in secret; and thy Father which seeth in secret shall reward thee openly." Now I know that he didn't mean to literally go into a closet and shut the door, but to close your eyes and shut out all negative thoughts and any thought that would distract you from communing with the Father. I thought back to the time when I was a little girl. I would go into the closet and shut the door when I was feeling overwhelmed with what was going on. I didn't know anything about the Bible then, but my heavenly Father was watching over me, and sent me in there to calm myself. What other explanation could there be?

With all the bad choices I'd made in the past, I suffered no lasting consequences. He was taking care of me until I found my way to him.

About four months after we moved into the duplex, I stopped seeing Dr. Klein, and two months later Darchele and I started attending church regularly. Darchele was then ten. She had wanted to go to Sunday school for a long time. Her friends at school had talked about God, and she wanted to know more. A while back, I'd tried taking her to a church not far from us, but I couldn't go to church yet, so I would drop her off and sleep in the car in the parking lot while I waited for her to come out. We didn't do that for very long. "...and a little child shall lead them." Isaiah 11:6.

A short time later, I felt ready to attend church but decided I couldn't because my budget was so tight, and I had no money to give to the church of my choice. It was funny how all sorts of things tried to keep me from attending church.

Regardless of all the arguments, one week I decided it was time to start going to church again. We got up Sunday morning and got ready and off we went to church. I got Darchele settled in Sunday school, which was in the basement, and went up to the church. It had been a while since I attended church, and I felt a little uncomfortable. Once the service started, I forgot all about my discomfort and concentrated on the message. When the service was over, several people greeted me, and they were all friendly. I gathered Darchele, and we went home.

We didn't have anything special planned that day that I can remember. What I do remember is that much later that afternoon I discovered something wonderful.

I had smoked for twenty-five years, from two to four packs a day. I had tried to quit many times without success. When I walked into church that Sunday, I had two packs of cigarettes in my purse. I walked out a non-smoker. I have had no desire for one since I left the church that morning and didn't realize it until later that afternoon. I don't know what it was, but something got to me that morning. I decided right then that I would never give less to church than what it had cost me to smoke. That solved my tithing problem. I also quit drinking that day. Never another cigarette or drink since then.

I remember one day not long after that my friends from the bank came over and I put two ashtrays on the table since they all smoked. When they left, I noticed all the ashtrays were full, but I didn't remember seeing any of them smoking. Wow, I was amazed. The healing was so complete that I didn't even see other people smoking anymore.

I was still working on my relationship with Darchele. I had begun to study the church lesson regularly, and slowly, I began to put into practice some of what I was learning. I realized I had to change the way I was seeing my daughter. I was still seeing the child I didn't like. I also needed to change my view of myself. Slowly, things started to change. Our relationship was becoming more relaxed, and we started having more fun again.

I joined the church and was later asked to teach the high school class in Sunday school. One Sunday, only one student showed up, and we had quite a conversation at the end of class. She had brought up something about there being some small children she didn't like, which made me think back to when my daughter was little and how much I disliked her at one time, and we talked about how we mended our relationship. She laughed and said it was hard to believe that the sweet, polite girl she knew could have possibly been the same girl I had just described.

Through my study, I had stopped seeing a lying, unreasonable, selfish, undisciplined child and began to see the child of God's creating, honest, reasonable, unselfish, and disciplined. There has been harmony and peace in our home ever since. Of course, we still had our spats, but it was different now. It was normal.

I always tried to make sure Darchele saw the better part of me. We both have things to work out; we are friends, and I love her dearly, but most of all, I like her now. I have finally found some measure of peace, and the cycle of abuse has stopped in my family. Things were getting better for me, and they had to get better for Darchele too.

Between my mom, Bill, and me, we made sure that Darchele had warm and loving holidays. I put aside my feelings so she wouldn't grow up with sad feelings about the holidays. One Christmas while we were in the duplex, I sold my piano so that I would have money for her Christmas presents.

We lived in the duplex for five years, the longest I had spent in one place thus far. We were happy there. Darchele was a good kid and always where she was supposed to be, so I never had to worry about her after school while I was at work. She did exceptionally well in school, unlike her mother, and for that, I am grateful. I never had to say anything about her homework, as that was a priority for her. Darchele was turning into a nice young lady.

When my younger brother was going into the service and needed his birth certificate, my mom told him it was in a box in the garage. While looking, he also found our parents' marriage license. They married in 1941. I was born in 1942, and Ken was two and a half years older than me. Ah-ha, something was wrong with this picture. It was during the war, and Dad was in the Army, so we figured that was why they got married late, but Ken was still his son. Everything we knew said that was true, and he even looked a little like him, so we let it drop.

While at the duplex, I had an opportunity to visit my mother's sister. It was the first time I was ever alone with her since I was a child. I decided to ask her about Ken's father. "Is my father Ken's father?"

"You mean they never told you kids?" my aunt responded.

"Told us what?" I replied.

She told me my mother had gotten pregnant with her high school boyfriend, and he wanted to marry her, but she didn't love him and wouldn't marry him, but decided to have the baby. Ken was one and a half when she married my father. He adopted Ken and swore everyone to secrecy. I was born a year later.

I told Ken's wife because I thought someone in his family should know the truth and did not want to do anything that might make my brother start drinking again. He had been sober for several years by then. I told her to tell him if she felt it would not bother him.

Several days later, I got a call from Ken. He said knowing that bastard, as he called our dad, was not his father was the best news ever. For him, it explained a lot about what had happened to him as a child. Well, I was his child, and he beat me too; explain that.

We should have figured something weird was going on, since normally, the first-born son gets the father's name, but it was our younger brother who was the third—Herb III. Ken and I did poorly in school, and Herb did very well, so maybe that was why he didn't get the beatings we did. I don't know, just a guess. Could have been that Herb was his flesh and blood son. Who knows?

Home Again with Mom and Bill

August 1990

Dear God,

I want to thank you for my mother. She may not have been there for me as a child, but has come through for me as an adult. She has been there every time I needed her. Bill is great too. He treats me like his own daughter.

WOW! I can't believe my daughter is going to a private boarding school and she loves it. I'm so happy for her.

I think everything is looking up now; my personal life has improved immensely. I still have lessons to learn, and I need to forgive. But did you have to make the lessons so hard?

Michele

I was at the top of my pay for the job I was doing at Bear Kat Products, and there was no room for advancement. I knew I needed more income than I was earning. I had been looking for a job for about two years. One day I found an ad in the paper that was just perfect for me. I applied and got the job.

This new job, on top of the normal five days at forty-eight hours per week, required me to work six days a week and twelve hours a day between Thanksgiving and New Year. I would need someone for Darchele during that time. I checked with my mother first, and she agreed that she and Bill would be glad to stay with us. They were already taking her back to Arkansas with them for the summers, so I didn't need a sitter then.

The new job was for a fancy jewelry store doing inventory control. The pay was much better than I was previously making, by almost double.

Since I started looking for this job, I had been working metaphysically on the idea of supply, learning that I could never be deprived of anything right for me to have. It was only right that I could supply Darchele and me with everything we needed to live, and not have to depend on others. I began to see the truth in that statement. God didn't create us to go without the things we needed, so I knew I would find a good job. We never did go without, as Mom and Bill were always there for us, even before I was able to provide our supply completely.

After I started that job, I found out one day that they had been looking for someone to fill this newly created spot for two years and never found what they were looking for in the applicants. Therefore, they decided they needed to change their ad. I found the new ad the first day it ran in the paper. I believe that job was mine from the beginning, and it was just waiting for me. When the time was right, we were brought together. I truly believe the way we think can make a big difference in our lives. If I'd thought I would never get what I was looking for, I would not have found that job.

We would have stayed in our duplex longer, but after five years, my mother and Bill wanted to move back to Michigan to be closer to family and asked us if we wanted to move in with them. I felt that with Darchele going into high school, it would be good to have a support system at home, so I agreed. Darchele was happy about it too. So, they got a house big enough for the four of us, and we left the duplex for their home to live with Mom and Bill once again.

Bill was such a great stepdad to me and grandfather for Darchele. Until Darchele was about twelve or thirteen, we'd lived in poverty. I made enough to feed us and put a roof over our heads but couldn't afford a car. Bill always made sure I had one. My mom loved to sew and made most of Darchele's clothes, and she always looked like she stepped out of a fashion magazine. They were always there for us, and they never judged. I was so grateful for their help. I sometimes think that my mom was trying to make up for all the abuse when I was a child, but it was never talked about.

I was no longer dating. I hadn't made good choices in men. I discovered that a man was not a requirement for a complete life anymore. I was earning enough now to support Darchele, and we were fine without one.

Moving back in with Mom and Bill turned out to be a good move. I was able to save some money since all I had to pay Mom and Bill was half the utilities and groceries. They owned the house and Mom said that was all they wanted.

Between Darchele's freshmen and sophomore years in high school, she went to a ranch out west with a group of kids that belonged to Adventure Unlimited, an organization she belonged to.

While there, she met many kids who were going to a private boarding school in Missouri and decided she wanted to go there. I told her I didn't have that kind of money. She asked if she could find a way, could she go. I said sure, never thinking she would find a way, but she did.

She called, and the school arranged to fly her out, at their expense, for an interview. They got her school records from the local school and my last three years of tax returns. They were impressed with her; she was a straight-A student and met all their criteria. She got a grant and finished high school there at no charge. I gave what I could, but it wasn't much.

I never let two months go by without flying down there for the weekend. At that time, a round trip plane fare was only $40, and I could afford that. My phone bills were huge, but that was okay. Darchele loved it there, and I was glad she was calling home regularly. With Darchele gone, I only paid one-third of the utilities and groceries. That was good for me. For the first time, I was able to pay for my own car.

The worst of my life was over, or so I thought. I was learning new ways to handle life situations, and it was making a big difference in my life.

I believed moving in with Mom and Bill would be a good thing, and it was. However, all wasn't well in my life yet; I still had challenges to meet and things to overcome. All this was leading to another phase of my life. My personal experience was improving, and now, my work life was hitting the pits. I was starting to learn how to handle adverse situations, but I had not mastered it yet. The great new job was starting to sour, and I would have never dreamed what was coming up next.

Cooper's

1987

Oh my gosh, God, what are you thinking?

I know, I know, how can I grow if my life is a bed of roses. The combination of these three men make one of my father. Did you put me here to overcome what he did to me?

I'm sorry I almost failed. Old emotions are coming back to the surface. The anger, the fear, the frustration keep coming up over and over again. Night after night, I go home and try to work out these feelings and replace them with Love. Many times, it doesn't work, but I'll never give up trying.

After almost four years of misery, I finally found the courage to stand up for myself. I put my mental foot down and said, "NO! I don't have to subject myself to this abuse." And why? Because you created me as your image and likeness, which means like you. All the Love, courage, and strength you have are mine as your child. I am strong, I took a stand at last, without fear of retribution, and it ended the abuse.

I am so grateful.

Thank You, God,
Michele

MICHELE FRANTZ

*"A gem is not polished without rubbing
nor a man perfected without trials."*
Confucius

I started at Cooper's in June 1987 while still in the duplex before we moved in with Mom and Bill.

I was hired to take responsibilities off Leo, the gemologist and department manager, so he could concentrate his efforts in other areas of more importance. I was to be a liaison between the vault (Leo, to be more specific), and all the other departments. In addition, I would be responsible for inventory control.

The owner's son, Dylan, was buying the store from his father. I would be controlling two inventories when that happened, one declining (the father's), and the other growing (the son's).

They warned me that Leo was difficult to get along with. That was an understatement.

Leo was on sick leave when I was hired. I floated from area to area learning the whole department. I got along well with everyone. Leo returned near the end of July 1987. By then, I had a good general knowledge of the operations of the office.

I sensed he was disturbed that, in his absence, someone new had been added to his department. After introductions, he rather gruffly said, "I'll get with you later." After a few conversations, he seemed to accept me. He would call me over to his work area and tell me all the negative things about each employee. He was trying to teach me how to handle them the same way he did. He felt all the salespeople were beneath him. He made comments like:

"Watch out for this one, he'll be nice to you only to get what he or she wants."

"Be careful of so and so because he just wants information about our department."

"This one or that will run right to Dylan with everything you say."

"It's best if you don't get friendly with any of them."

"We once had a girl in your position who used to talk to Bill (the manager) all the time. You'll notice she's not here anymore."

"Just remember I'm the one who has control of your raises."

This was the message I was getting: "Everyone outside the vault is the enemy, and your income depends on whether you keep me happy." He succeeded. I was concerned.

Leo made it very clear that the vault was his private domain, and if I crossed him, he would make life so miserable that I would no longer have a job. He had no idea that in all my past jobs, I worked in constant fear of being fired. I thought that eventually, my employers would discover I was a fake, and not as smart as they thought, and not worth the pay. I thought that I would eventually do something incredibly stupid and get fired.

At first, I didn't see a problem, and I didn't believe anything Leo said about my co-workers; they didn't seem like little devils to me. I liked everyone—some better than others, but all friendly people. I was enjoying my new job. Leo's training methods were a bit odd, but I managed to learn what I needed to know.

After a while, when he would see a salesperson talking to me, about business I might add, he would scream at me across the room that I had work to do, and I didn't have time to do things for the salespeople. After the salesperson would leave, he would let me know that was for the benefit of the salesperson, so they would know that they couldn't get away with taking advantage of the vault staff. Screaming at me sure seemed a funny way of communicating with the salesperson. Though I didn't like it, I learned to live with his childish outbursts at me, to get a message through to someone else.

Eventually, I was given more authority in the vault, and Leo moved me over to the work area directly across from him, where there was only a glass window between us. There was an opening at the desktop level with a sliding door about four inches high where he could pass jobs through for me to do. There we sat, face-to-face eight to ten hours a day. In his mind, we were now great buddies.

In January 1988, Dylan told us that he would be buying the store from his father, and we had until the end of February to come up with a new stock number format for his new inventory. This was the position I was hired for; to manage a dual inventory. I set up the new stocking system, and he was happy.

At this point, Dylan started dealing directly with me, and that was when the real trouble began. The chain of command had been broken.

This disturbed Leo. He had lost control over part of my work because he didn't know what I was doing. Every time he tried to do something the old way, I tried, as nicely as possible, to explain the new way, and he'd be angry with me for weeks.

Leo didn't like Mr. Cooper's new bookkeepers, because he thought they were trying to cheat Dylan out of money. So, once a month, when we got together to balance, we would try to do it when Leo wasn't around.

Leo did everything he could to prevent me from interacting with other employees, even when it was work-related. Co-workers discovered they had to meet with me when he wasn't around.

One day Dylan took me to lunch to discuss some business items we hadn't been able to get to because he had been too busy. After the business at hand was finished, he started in on my performance. All the while he was telling me how good I was and that he wouldn't trust anyone else with my job, in the same breath, he was telling me how bad I was. I don't know how he could make a judgment on how I spent my time when he was in the vault for such a small amount of time each week. He also said he wanted me to stop talking, to set an example for the other girls in the vault. I was very confused when I returned from lunch. I couldn't tell whether I had been praised or reprimanded. I began to wonder if Leo had been saying things to him that weren't true. I felt physically ill, and I went home.

In October 89, Dylan took me out to lunch again, this time to discuss my long past due pay increase. The discussion went better this time. He agreed to give me half my raise now and make it retroactive back to June 89 and the other half on completion of a project he wanted me to do. All I had to do was turn it in, and I would get the other half of my raise, even if he never did anything with it. There was one stipulation; I must not tell anyone what I was doing, not even Leo, so I had to do this on my own time at home.

The project was to put in writing a plan to restructure Cooper's in such a way as to keep everyone happy and be a more efficient company. I had many ideas, but what I ultimately ended up doing was nothing like what I thought in the beginning.

Several weeks went by, and for some reason, I just couldn't get started. Every time I looked at Leo, I felt guilty. We were getting along quite well at the time, he would talk to me about how he wanted the vault to run, and I couldn't even respond to him because I knew I was giving Dylan ideas of my own.

Finally, I went to Dylan and told him I didn't feel I could do his project behind Leo's back; it felt like I was cheating on a test. Immediately Dylan said that is not what he meant, but he wasn't sure if he had explained it to Leo, so he would take him out to lunch right away and tell him about the project. I thought to myself, "Dylan let's be honest now, that *was* what you meant." That very day they went out to lunch, and I felt comfortable that all was well.

All was not well. I was sorry that I ever agreed to do the project in the first place. I felt Dylan was way out of line even asking me to do it, since Leo was supposed to be my supervisor. Bribing me with a pay increase was just plain wrong. Chain of command was definitely all out of whack, and it was causing a lot of trouble.

When Leo found out I was working on a flow chart for the vault, he made it very clear that I didn't know enough, nor was I smart enough, to do it. He said, "You do what you have to do, and I'll tear it apart."

As time went on, things deteriorated. Leo and I fluctuated back and forth between being buddies and bitter enemies. I felt sorry for him. I knew that he was not angry with me but with the situation. I took my lead from him. When he was angry, and he didn't need a reason (sounds like my dad), I would stay out of his way.

I believe it was sometime in October 89 that they hired Cathy to replace David, Leo's assistant, who had quit. I liked Cathy, and sometimes it got to me when I heard Leo pumping her full of all the negative garbage he used to tell me. (Here let me teach you how to hate and distrust the people you work with.)

The project was completed and turned in at the end of January 90. I had a meeting with Dylan and Bill, and they were both impressed with the project I presented. They agreed with the content of the written report and seemed to like the flow charts I had done, and the reports were distributed to the department heads.

I was trying to change my thinking about how to handle situations with Leo, but when he would start, I would fall back into old patterns of feeling and acting. I was a child again. I felt like I was being belittled by my father, that I was stupid, and this was my fault. If I were better at this or that, this wouldn't be happening. Reacting as a child was hard to change.

Repeatedly Leo would come after me for things I had nothing to do with and try to blame them on me. Somehow, everything was always my fault.

When the workload would get heavy for the other girls, and I had time, I was always there to help. When my workload would get heavy, and I would ask Leo if I could get some help, he would reply in his usual degrading manner, "Well, I guess you'll just have to work a little harder, won't you." Once I specifically asked if Ann could help me with something, and he said, "No, I have something else I want her to do."

Talk about putting a computer in our department began. Dylan ordered some software, borrowed the hardware, and asked me to test it.

Leo had wanted the computer when he thought it was an impossible dream, but now that it was sitting in his office, he was not happy at all, so I stayed out of his way.

Bill tried to get Leo and me into a conversation about the computer, and I was to work with him on what it would do. Leo waved me off with, "Go on, go on; just do what you have to do. You take care of it." When he looked at me, all he could see was a king-sized computer, and he hated me. He could not separate me from the work I was doing.

I was letting Leo get the best of me, and I had gotten angry and said things to Dylan I wish I could take back. I had let people at work see a side of me even I didn't like. Things were getting out of control.

I had been learning many things in church about how to see these things in a different light, so they would not get to me, but I wasn't able to demonstrate this yet. I tried as hard as I could, but the emotion bubbled up, and I got my feelings hurt and got angry and offended. I was feeling stronger in some ways because I was slowly starting to speak up for myself. I didn't always go as far as I should have before the fear set in, and I stopped. Progress was slow.

OUT OF DARKNESS, INTO THE LIGHT

I talked to Dylan about the situation with Leo, and he assured me that he would speak to Leo. Apparently, he did, as Leo started being nice to me. I had hopes that maybe the whole thing was over, and we could get down to the business of doing our jobs.

Little did I know that was a put-on; he was just biding his time. He was waiting for the right time to stick the knife in and twist it. He took me out for a business lunch one day.

He started with, "Just who is your boss?"

"Dylan signs my paychecks, and you run the vault."

He asked how Bill fit into this. I responded, "Bill is in on most of my dealings with Dylan." Then he wanted to know why I went crying to Dylan because of him. I said, "You gave me no other choice."

I started to get upset and was unable to hold back the tears. I felt trapped sitting in a restaurant like that with nowhere to go. I couldn't even get up and leave, since he drove and I didn't have my car. He said he didn't want to upset me.

"Well, I *am* upset," I said.

Then he started in on the flowchart project and asked why I didn't keep him better informed about what I was doing. Well, he didn't want to hear about it when I was working on it. I told him I was tired of being Dylan's whipping boy, and if he didn't like something Dylan did, he should not take it out on me. For everything else, he accused me of at lunch, my responses were as follows: That is not my responsibility. I do not have any control over that. I didn't do it. I don't know anything about it.

When he was all finished beating me up, he said, "Let's wipe the slate clean and start over."

I thought, "Sure, now that you got in all your digs, and let out all your hostility, and I'm completely frustrated because I had to sit here and say nothing, because you're my boss and it would be considered insubordination to tell you what I really think, sure now let's wipe the slate clean. NEVER. There's so much chalk dust on this slate, it will never come clean. What gives you the right to treat me this way?"

There was a lack of communication between Leo and Dylan, causing Leo's hostility toward me. I knew that and I felt for Leo, but I was caught in the middle, and that wasn't right.

The proverbial straw that broke the camel's back started on Wednesday, June 27, 1990. I made an insignificant mistake and hadn't removed an envelope containing a couple of small, broken stones, which was stapled to the paperwork before sending it up to bookkeeping. Leo didn't say anything right away, as was par for him; he was waiting for the perfect time to step in and let me have it.

One of my co-workers was there when Leo found out and got to me before he did. When Leo returned to the vault, I wasn't sure whether to approach him or wait and see what would happen. He finally said, "Michele, I wish you would be more careful about what you send up to bookkeeping."

"Yes, I know about it. Liza told me, and I will be more careful."

He said no more. I was shocked but pleased.

Liza called later to see what happened and I told her. She said, "Wow, that's scary." We laughed, hung up, and forgot about it.

Later he came down on me hard. Thinking he must be talking about the broken stones I sent up to bookkeeping in error, I said, "You mean the broken stones?"

"What difference does it make if they are broken, they are still money," he screamed at me. He was awful, and when I left, I cried all the way home that night. Once again, I was beaten for doing my job right, except for those broken stones, of course, which were actually worthless.

The next day he was being his usual unpleasant self and quizzing me on all sorts of things that were going on in the vault, and after he had finished, he handed me some paperwork. I was puzzled about the things he handed me and started to say something when I decided to drop it. It was clear he didn't want any of my input. However, it was too late. As I turned to leave, he said in the most sarcastic tone of voice, "Whatever *you* want, Michele, however *you* think it should be done, Michele."

That was all it took. I was so angry and felt I might say something I would be sorry for later. I was ready to explode. The man was utterly impossible. I bent over backwards to do what he wanted, but nothing worked.

I couldn't get out the door fast enough. By the time my car reached the street, I let out a scream that nearly broke my eardrums, followed by repeated cries of, "I hate him."

I sobbed all the way home in the car. I could barely see the road to drive. When I got home, my poor mother and stepfather got an ear full. I said the most hateful things about Leo. I said I wished he were dead and more. I hated feeling that way and just wanted it to all go away, but it wouldn't. I cried myself to sleep that night.

I was still reacting like a child. I needed to do something about this. I had to start putting into action all the new things I was learning, but it was hard.

In the morning, I thought I was okay, so I got ready and went to work. I couldn't stand being in the same room as Leo. After about an hour, I went to the restroom and couldn't return to the vault. I left and went home.

Almost the entire time I worked at Cooper's, I would go home night after night to work through my anger and turn it into forgiveness. I used to smile all the time at work, but now I had to force the smiles most of the time.

When I started, I was happy, then the happiness turned into misery, and the misery into anger, and the anger to fear. I was afraid to talk to Leo. I didn't trust him. He would turn on me for any reason, just like my dad.

I knew I couldn't go to another job with anger in my heart. I had to work it out, so I had something good to take with me to a new job. My motives for leaving had to be other than anger.

Dylan decided he needed to make a change since he guessed he was about to lose me. He made Bill supervisor over the vault staff, which did not include Leo. And of course, Leo blamed me for this, and he was right.

It was October, and at last Leo was speaking to me again, and I didn't feel intimidated. I think he had finally given up the battle.

By March 1991, I understood that Bill was not much of a supervisor either. He never followed through or backed me up on anything.

I guess this was the last straw. I couldn't trust Leo. I couldn't trust Bill, and I never could trust Dylan. With no trust in my superiors, this job was lost. I had hit bottom, and there was no place to go but up.

I felt better once I started to look seriously for a new job; just making the decision relieved the stress. Those people were doing the best they could. They did not know any better, or they would do better.

On April 18, Dylan laid off Bill and five others. Cathy, Leo's new assistant gemologist, quit. I can't say that I blame her. At the time that happened, Leo was home on sick leave recuperating from a heart attack. It was not surprising, since he put an awful lot of negative stress on himself.

Dylan said that my position in the vault would remain unchanged. I would still be vault coordinator, such as it was. He said that he wanted me to do whatever I had to do to make vault-processing run more smoothly and quickly. The workload was bound to increase for those of us left. Therefore, we worked a little harder. Everything seemed to be okay, and I was determined that things would work out when Leo came back. Little did I know what lay ahead.

On May 3rd, the Friday before Leo was to return, I started to react. All the old feelings came rushing back. I didn't want to be there when that man came back. He was not a nice person, and based on the past, I knew I could only expect him to take revenge on me for what had occurred in his absence. As far as he was concerned, it was my fault he was relieved of managing the vault, and now he was to be my boss again. I wanted to scream, "Why me? Why am I being tortured like this? Why am I being put back in prison? What is my crime?"

I needed to STOP thinking like this; why me was victim talk. I needed to stop acting like a victim if I wanted to stop responding like a child. I couldn't afford to quit without another job, so I was stuck there.

On May 7, 1991, Leo returned, and I was not far from wrong. On Thursday, he finally sat me down and informed me that if he was here, he would run the vault. Fine, I knew he would be my boss again, but what he said wasn't a statement but a threat. He very calmly told me how we would now run the vault. Then he said he wanted no stress and along with inventory control, I was to supervise the area that handled setting stones, repairs, sizings, etc.

Dylan said the handcuffs were off and Leo put them back on. I was now just a puppet on his string, at the mercy of his temper and nastiness, just like before.

Thursday afternoon and evening, I was in such an emotional state that I couldn't go to work on Friday. I tried hard Friday to turn my thinking around and accept what was happening. I needed to bide my time until I found new employment.

The first thing he said to me Saturday as I was sorting out the previous day's leftovers was, "Michele, go do the check-in," as if I was so stupid as to consider anything else since there were two full boxes. Later he brought over some new work, special orders, and said, "Here do these."

I guess that was an example of how to play the game now. Say nothing, and think nothing, and do as I was told. Leo sounded like my father. "Don't think. I'll tell you what to think."

On Sunday, I knew I had to talk to Dylan on Monday. That was not going to be easy, but it had to be done. Tears or no tears, I must speak now or shut my mouth and bear the abuse.

I talked with Dylan, and he again took Leo out to lunch. Things improved for a while, but Leo never did speak to me the way he should have.

I was getting so frustrated by everything and decided it was time to stop and pray. I needed God's help.

Dear God,

Help me see your creation. I am caught in the mist, and seeing the world through unclear eyes. I know in my heart that I am your image and likeness. Please help me to understand the truth of this, so I can also see my fellow man in your image.

I know as your image, failure cannot be a part of me that I reflect your qualities of confidence and strength, that I am fearless, stable, and triumphant. I am secure in your care. That is my true identity.

In the Lord's Prayer, it states, "Thy kingdom come. Thy will be done on earth, as it is in heaven," and this tells me I can experience heaven on earth. I do not have to live in constant turmoil.

I am listening, I am ready, and I know you will show me the way.

With Love,
Your child Michele

There was another incident, and I do not remember all the details, but what I do remember made me feel good. I had at last done the right thing. Leo was his usual self and was hollering at me about something when it occurred to me that as God's image, I reflected his courage and strength, that I was not a child anymore, and I did not have to sit there and take his abuse. I felt the fear lift; I stood up, turned my back, and headed for the door. He jumped up and shouted, "Don't you turn your back on me."

I heard him move and turned just in time to see him catch himself. He had raised his hand and was about to hit me. I looked him straight in the eyes and said nothing; there was nothing to say. I think the look on my face said it all. I could see by the look on his face that he knew something had changed, and he could no longer bully me.

I felt compassion for this man, maybe even love. He was doing the best he could, but for me, all the anger, the frustration, and wanting to strike back were gone. I was free. I was able to see past the angry man, to the man God created, the good man in his likeness. Now that didn't mean I suddenly liked him. I didn't like his human personality, but I knew under that was a good man, and he just hadn't been able to bring that man out. Just as I had not been able to bring out the goodness in me at times, so how could I judge him?

I think I had just learned what it meant to love your enemy. I was starting to understand not only my relationship but also everyone's relationship with God. We are all here in this experience struggling to find the goodness, both in ourselves and in others. Although some of us are doing a better job of it, that doesn't change the fact that we were all created equal as God's beloved children. That is our spiritual essence, and when I discovered that, and understood what it meant, it changed me. I now see everything around me differently.

I just turned then and left the vault. Leo knew it was over. He never talked to me disrespectfully again. That was when I truly forgave my father. I let go of my hate, my anger, my fears, and my wanting revenge. I was free to love.

That was my awakening, the turning point in my life. I was starting to understand God's creation versus our creation. We make the mess, and as a loving, caring parent, he guides us through redemption.

Here is a quote from *Miscellaneous Writings*, by Mary Baker Eddy.

"We have no enemies. Whatever envy, hatred, revenge—the most remorseless motives that govern mortal mind—whatever these try to do shall 'work together for good to them that love God.'

Why?

Because He has called His own, armed them, equipped them, and furnished them defenses impregnable. Their God will not let them be lost; and if they fall they shall rise again, stronger than before the stumble. The good cannot lose their God, their help in times of trouble. If they mistake the divine command, they will recover it, countermand their order, retrace their steps and reinstate His order, more assured to press on safely. The best lesson of their lives is gained by crossing swords with temptation, with fear and the besetments of evil; insomuch as they thereby have tried their strength and proven it; insomuch as they have found their strength made perfect in weakness, and their fear is self-immolated."

It was hard to believe it was almost over. On June 25, 1991, I accepted a new position. I was a short-timer now.

When I started looking for another job, the few at work who knew told me it would be hard because Cooper's held its employees with "golden handcuffs." They said he pays so well that it is hard to find another job that pays as well. I found another job making a little more than I was making there. However, the pay was not the issue. I just needed to start over in a fresh atmosphere.

I had worked metaphysically on the idea of supply again. God never leaves his children in want. Now, that is simply put; there is a lot more to understanding the Principle behind it. I wished I had done the proper metaphysical work while at Cooper's. I felt like I did everything wrong. I let Cooper's drag me down to their level. I even swore a few times, which I hadn't done in years. I was overcome with anger many times. However, in the

OUT OF DARKNESS, INTO THE LIGHT

end, I gained some self-respect at last. With God's help, I finally stood up for myself. However, I still had many lessons to learn.

My new job started, and it was a challenge, but I was better prepared to handle situations when they came up.

A. R. Mason, Inc.

July 1991

Hello God,

I can't thank you enough for all your help. I am finally finding my way. This is the best job I have ever had. It has provided me with many opportunities to learn and grow in my understanding of my relationship with you.

Learning how to let go and listen for that "still small voice" has helped me to live my life according to your law of Love. I am learning to trust my instincts and intuition, as that is another way you communicate with me.

I saw the proof of your protection and love many times during this period of my life. You are my salvation. Jesus showed us the way: all I need to do is follow him. Thank you for sending him.

Michele

A new chapter of my life had started. I accepted a job doing Inventory Control and Purchasing for a company that distributed fluid hydraulic parts and builds hydraulic devices. When I started, a few individuals resented a new employee coming in and changing everything. I could understand that. As I did my metaphysical work one at a time, these individuals found new jobs and quit. Their replacements were easy to get along with and cooperative.

It was a difficult start, but after four months, I finally started to see the light at the end of the tunnel.

I had not solved all my problems at Cooper's, so I had to work them out at Mason's. However, I did it differently. I finally learned to stop saying things like, "What's wrong with me? Why do these things keep happening to me?" That was thinking of myself as a victim of circumstances and only made me feel helpless and powerless.

While studying the textbook at church, I learned the power of thought. I was trying to change the way I was thinking. I was refusing to let in those confused, fearful thoughts, and replaced them with powerful "can do" thoughts. I found it worked. I had to take these challenges and turn them into opportunities to learn new ways of facing adversity. My fears started to subside, allowing me to speak up more.

One thing I learned from Mr. Cooper's bookkeeper was that an immediate answer to every question was not necessary. She was intelligent, and never had a problem saying, "Let me think about it and get back to you," or "Let me do some research and get back to you." There was no shame in doing that. It even made me feel better about myself. It was intelligent, not stupid.

My father always made me feel stupid if I couldn't come up with an answer the minute he asked a question. Because of that, I made many mistakes in later years trying to answer questions when I didn't have good answers. Now I knew better.

The workload was overwhelming when I started. I couldn't seem to get everything done, and no one could answer my questions. I had to figure things out for myself, which was not bad, but it took time, of which I had little.

I spoke with Evan Mason, son of the owner and VP of operations, and Janet, the office manager and an accountant, twice with my concerns that important things were not getting done on a timely basis, and I needed help. Bea, the woman who had the job before me, came back part-time and did the order entry, which helped, but it wasn't enough. I'd worked through my lunch hour ever since I started, and many times stayed late or came in early to help get the work done.

Right after I started, Evan fired Dan, who worked the order desk, and shortly after that, Jack had heart surgery and decided to retire instead of coming back to work. So now, we were down two people on the order desk, which usually had three.

As a funny aside, the people in my work area swore a lot. One of the girls noticed I didn't swear and said something about it. I told her I never felt the need to. She said to give myself some time, and I would be swearing like the rest of them. Time went by, and one day, I noticed the cussing had stopped. For that I was grateful.

After quite a while, they hired Anna for the order desk. We got off to a bad start. She had not been there two weeks when I started snapping at her. I do not remember why. I talked to her one day, which in the past was something I would have been afraid to do. I apologized for snapping and we worked out our differences. Things were fine after that.

At first, it took all the courage I had to confront someone when we were having a problem, but it got easier. I discovered that the sky would not fall if I did it; in fact, it made things better. On the rare occasion that it didn't, I at least felt better for making an effort.

I thought I had to solve all the problems, and the harder I tried, the worse things got. I even went to Evan one day in tears, saying, "I don't understand why I'm not getting the work done. What is different now?" I hated crying at work; it was so unprofessional. He said he didn't know and would work with me for a while and see what he could do. That was unrealistic, as he had no time for me, nor did Janet. I had to solve the problem myself.

I blamed everyone else for the trouble. If people didn't make so many mistakes, I would not need to spend so much time fixing them, etcetera, etcetera, etcetera. All the customer orders passed through my office, so I could process the purchasing. That is where I caught the mistakes.

It finally occurred to me that what I was *feeling* was my fault. "I of mine own self do nothing." I wasn't letting go of the problem so God could set it right. I needed to listen for the "still small voice" to speak to me. I knew I had to let go and relax and look at everything calmly. When I did, the ideas (the still small voice of God talking to me) began to flow. Within a week, things began to be set right. Not perfect yet, but turning around quite nicely. I felt one hundred percent better. The stress eased, and I was smiling again.

I began to see what one of the problems was; their inventory was completely out of control. In the past, they never had anyone who understood inventory management, so they did not know how to do it. That was why it was taking me so much time. I was actually doing inventory control.

My last two jobs were inventory control—twelve years' experience. Trained by a man who had a degree in inventory management, I felt confident I could get things under control.

Evan called me into the conference room one day, and I sat with him, Janet, and Mr. Mason, the owner. I told them things were much better, that I was figuring out where the bottlenecks were, and breaking them up. I also told them I would get their inventory in balance. They asked how I planned to do that, given their inventory had never been in balance. I told them with hard work. I said, "You give me a starting point, and I will balance it and keep it in balance." I needed a fresh physical inventory count to start. It was June, and inventory was usually done at year-end, but he agreed to have a count done at that time.

The physical count was completed and entered into the computer. More than fifty percent of the inventory was out of balance. In the past, they took the new counts and did nothing. I can't believe they called that balancing the inventory. That was only the first step.

I had a team go back to the warehouse and recount all the items that were not in balance with the computer. Many of the discrepancies were miscounts. Other differences were because the computer hadn't been updated with certain kinds of transactions.

I did some investigating and discovered about 150 customer returns stuck on the shelves with no follow-up or adjustment in the computer. Some of them were very old. When the customers complained that they had not received a credit, accounting would credit them without making sure the product had been returned and the inventory adjusted.

It took a long time to take care of those returns. Some were so old we could not send them back to the vendor. Some were "made to order," and the vendors would not take them back. Mason's should not have taken them back either. There were many dollars lost because of this.

Evan was shocked; he could not believe this had happened, and no one knew about it. The guy in the warehouse should have been on top of this; instead, he stashed the returns wherever he could fit them and did nothing. He was fired. In the future, accounts receivable could not credit a customer order without approval from inventory control. We had to make sure the returned goods were correctly processed before the customer was credited.

Six months after the first physical inventory, it was time to count again. Of course, the employees didn't like it. They felt like they had just done inventory. No one likes to do physical inventory, and I couldn't blame them; it was not my favorite thing either, but it needed to be done.

Again, it was out of balance quite a bit. A team once again did recounts. Many of them, like before, were miscounts. When done, we were still out of balance, and with some investigation, the computer was corrected, and some were written off. Mr. Mason, Evan, and Janet were thrilled, as was I. We had a good starting point.

The new warehouse manager was great; in fact, Evan nicknamed him Saint Dennis. With the previous manager, orders were sometimes taking up to two weeks to get shipped and management was not aware this was not necessary, and not a good thing. Dennis and I worked so well together that we were able to get orders shipped next day unless they requested same-day shipping.

Determined that the next year would be different, I set out with the help of Dennis, who was responsible for the physical location of the inventory, to bring this inventory under control. He was great to work with. I might mention he is still with Mason's also. He has been there almost as long as I have.

A year went by and it was time to see what all our hard work had accomplished. We had just entered the 1992 physical inventory into the computer and were ready to print out the variance report. Janet, the controller, came to me and said that some of the information we needed had somehow been lost and we could not get an accurate variance report, that the totals would be wrong, and the report would be useless.

I'd looked forward to this day for a whole year and felt I had been deprived of the fruits of my labor. When Janet left my office, I wanted to put my head on my desk and cry, but instead, I closed my office door and reached for my church textbook which I kept in my desk drawer. Now was the time to pray. I let the book open at random, and the first thing I saw was, "Accidents are unknown to God, or immortal Mind and we must leave the mortal basis of belief and unite with the one Mind, in order to change the notion of chance to the proper sense of God's unerring direction and thus bring out harmony. Under divine providence there can be no accidents, since there is no room for imperfection in perfection."

I began to see this was only a belief; that someone had, by chance, accidentally pushed a wrong button on the computer and lost important information. For a moment, the thought crossed my mind—this was not a misplaced button; it was irretrievable. What followed was a firm, NO! I was not going to give in to this.

Nothing can be added to or taken from God's creation, and no loss can occur from trusting God with our desires. Then another quote from the Bible came to mind. "The battle is not yours, but God's...Set yourselves, stand ye still, and see the salvation of the Lord."

I knew it was time to get myself out of the way. I had taken my stand on the side of Truth, and it was time to let God do his work. I felt a sense of peace and knew it was time to put away my book, open my door, and go back to work.

About an hour later, Janet came into my office again, and I could tell by the look on her face that "all was well." The thought (God's still small voice) had come to her to check one more thing, and she discovered the problem and corrected it, and as we spoke the report was printing. God speaks to us all; we just need to listen.

I am pleased to say the variance report was only about half an inch thick this time compared to the three inches from the previous two inventories, and about eighty to eighty-five percent was inactive parts, which were an easy fix, and the rest wouldn't take long at all to resolve. There were fewer miscounts, and as the years went by the employees started counting better. Knowing that if they didn't, they would have to recount, so they did it right the first time.

I walked around the rest of the day with a grin on my face, and I'm sure no one there knew why. Yes, I got the report I wanted, but what excited me was that once again, I had witnessed God's complete control and love for his creation.

I loved my job. Problems came up and were quickly resolved. One day I noticed I was walking with my head held up. I wasn't looking at the floor anymore. I was starting to see I was not stupid, and I was a good person. I had nothing to fear.

When I had been there about five years, they hired Mark for the order desk. He was a good worker and knew the product line. We got along well.

I was a morning person, and he was not, so I didn't talk to him much until after he had his coffee and settled in. He referred to me as "Rebecca of Sunnybrook Farms," and I called him "Oscar the Grouch."

He never talked about his personal life, so we only talked about the news and things going on at work. I didn't think that was unusual for a man.

While working at Mason's, Darchele went through college. She was getting a degree in computer science and was happily sharing what she was learning with me. I learned a great deal about computers and put it to use at work.

My stepfather became ill about this time, and I helped my mom care for him until he passed on December 14, 2001. Running my mom back and forth to the nursing home and keeping my job going, kept me busy, but I made it.

I received a call from my father's third wife a few weeks after Bill passed away. My father was in the hospital on life support, and if we kids wanted to see him, we should come now. I contacted my brothers, and of course, Ken didn't care and wouldn't go, but my younger brother said he wanted to go, so I went with him.

While there, the doctor said he could cut back the morphine, and he would become more alert, but I had no desire to talk to him. Herb did not want him to suffer, so he said no as well. He never knew we were there. His wife asked us about removing life support, and we all agreed that it would be okay.

Herb and I left. It took Dad several days to pass after removing life support. He was gone, and though I had forgiven him, I felt nothing. I felt much more when my stepfather passed. But with my father, I went back to work as if nothing had happened.

Although I was making more money now, it still wasn't enough to put a child through college. Darchele managed to take control of this and go through college on grants and scholarships, which didn't need repayment, except for her senior year when she went to a different college, and she had to get a loan. There were still lots of other costs, but I decided not to worry about it. I just ran up my charge account and figured I would pay it off after she graduated.

Much to my surprise, God came through with my supply again. The company put in a new computer system. Janet and I were responsible for getting it up and running. We had our work cut out for us. First, we had to learn the system, then train all the other employees how to use it. It was work, but I enjoyed it.

Then came the day of change over, and we entered all the open customer orders, vendor orders, payables, and receivables into the new computer system. We went from a mainframe to a PC network, so we all had new computers on our desks, and we all worked to get the data input.

PC networks were relatively new at that time, and what I was learning from Darchele put me miles ahead of the others in the office. I became their go-to person for computer problems.

At this time, my relationship with Mark, the young man on the order desk, changed drastically. Like Leo at Cooper's, he didn't like the new computer system, and he turned on me. Like Leo, he saw me as a big computer and didn't like me anymore. That saddened me as we had gotten along so well before.

When I would hand him some paperwork, he would throw it in the wastepaper basket to show his contempt for me and the way things were going. I caught him a couple of times taking it back out, so I knew it never stayed there and didn't worry about it.

He never talked to me again unless it was job-related and he had to. When I spoke to him, I would get one-word answers if that. I didn't understand how a computer could turn someone into such a miserable person.

His cubicle was right outside my office door, so I could hear everything he said. He was rude to the customers, which bothered me. Some customers would even try to get me to take their order. Sometimes I would if it was a product I knew about. I was not technical, so for a lot of the product lines, I couldn't be of help.

One day it really got to me. He slammed the phone on the counter, and said rude things that I knew the customer heard because as far as it appeared he had not put the phone on hold, but I could have been wrong.

I turned to God to get me through this. I closed my office door, took my Bible from my desk drawer, opened it at random, and put my finger on the page. That was something I did a lot, and it always helped.

What I read was, "Mark the perfect *man*, and behold the upright: for the end of *that* man *is* peace." Ps 37:37. My God, I almost laughed. Now I know it didn't mean Mark as a man's name, but it meant to *see* the perfect man. That was all I needed to read. I was not seeing Mark correctly. I had to change my perception of who he was. Well, that few minutes in my office did not change Mark, but it did change me. His behavior no longer disturbed me.

There is more than one type of prayer, and in this case, I wasn't asking God for things but listening for his voice to give me the ideas that would change the way I saw things, then things would happen. "Not my will, but thine, be done." This was much different from how I reacted to Leo, with anger and tears and a lot of frustration. I was finally past that kind of reaction to adverse situations.

I had been looking for a way to express my own unique identity. I was learning that we all have a special talent. I didn't know what mine was until I discovered Crystal Reports, an integrated application that came with our new company software, Macola.

Macola didn't have a reporting system that satisfied Evan, but with Crystal Reports, we could design our own reports. That made him happy, but there was no one in the company that had a clue how to use it.

The company that sold us the software created a few reports for Evan to get us started. It turned out I was the only one in the company interested in learning it. I took those reports and taught myself how to create some simple reports. As time went on, I kept getting better at it. By the time Evan asked me to enroll in a class, the instructors asked me some questions and placed me in the intermediate class; I was better than a beginner but not quite ready for the advanced class yet. ☺ I had found my niche. I loved Crystal. It allowed me to be creative and do things I never dreamed I could. For me, it wasn't working; it was fun.

Speaking of dreams, this was amazing. There was a report that Evan wanted, but the company who sold us Crystal and supported it said it could not be done. Well, they also told us when we purchased it that anything in Macola, we could pull into Crystal and report on it. Well, everything Evan wanted was in Macola, so I went to work on it.

It was all I thought about for a couple weeks. I barely got my other work done. Nothing I tried worked. I was about to give up when it happened. One night after work when I was getting ready for bed, I was mentally going over everything I had done, trying to figure out why it was not working. That night I dreamed the full report, start to finish, and it became clear what I had to do. I could hardly wait to get to work in the morning.

When I got to work, I started putting the report together, just a little at a time. After each little bit, I would run the report to see if it worked, and it did. When I reached a certain point, I went to Evan with what I had. He was thrilled; he was going to get his report.

I was excited. I probably spent over a hundred hours on this report. It had about one hundred and fifty sub-reports (reports within reports), and hundreds of formulas. When done, it did everything

Evan wanted and more. Using Crystal, I was now auditing the daily entry in all departments to make sure they were entering things in the right fields.

Inventory was so under control now that I had time to work with Crystal. The more I did, the more Evan wanted. He was excited about the kinds of information he could get. The next thing I knew, I was working about sixty-five hours a week making reports. I was set up to do my overtime work remotely from home, so it made it easier. I could go home, eat dinner, and go back to work from home. It was great!

I made reports for customer service, purchasing, inventory, accounting, the shop, and so on. These reports, with the click of a button, would supply them with current up-to-the-minute data on whatever they needed. Some reports were run daily, some weekly, some monthly and some even yearly for projections for the next year's business. Evan also had one he ran hourly, to see orders entered into the system so far that day. I told him that one day, he would drive himself crazy doing that.

Mr. Mason now owned four companies, and I was reporting for all four. I designed well over fifteen hundred reports; maybe closer to two thousand. Some were easy because some employee would say, "I would like that report, but could you switch these columns around and add this or that."

In those cases, I would just do a "save as" on the original report, rename it for the other employee, and make the changes.

When they realized we could make forms with Crystal, they had me create forms that we had been ordering from an outside source, like purchase orders and invoices. We used to load the forms into the printer and then print the data on them, and now the form and the data printed at the same time, no more loading forms in the printer. Everything printed on plain paper and even printed in color.

I took several college courses to help me with my job and aced them all. If I had applied myself in high school and gone to college, there's no telling where I would be today—certainly making more money.

I was making more in overtime than in my regular pay. That went on for three years. I paid off all of Darchele's college expenses and all my other bills, including my car. For the first time in my adult life, I was debt free—what a wonderful feeling.

At this point, the company put me on salary because I was making too much in overtime. Lucky for me, everything was paid off, and this was perfect timing. Now I could start putting something away for my retirement. I was getting a late start, so I put away every penny I could.

When Darchele was in college, she met Tony and fell in love. After she graduated, she and Tony were married, bought a house, and stayed in Missouri.

After my stepfather passed away, I decided if I ever wanted to spend any quality time with my daughter, I needed to move to Missouri to be near her.

I told my mom what I wanted to do, and she said she could live anywhere and was willing to move with me. When my stepfather passed, my mother and I stayed together since it did not make any sense to live separate.

I'd saved up the equivalent of a few months' salary, so I had some extra money. With no bills, my expenses would be low. There would only be monthly bills like insurance for the car, and so forth.

I didn't want to quit my job at Mason's, but I wanted to be near Darchele, so I turned in my notice. I told them it would take a while to sell the house, since the selling market wasn't good right then. We figured we had about six months. I said I would give them a month's notice, giving them a chance to find someone. They were sorry to see me go but understood.

Friends and co-workers told me I was making a mistake, finding a job at sixty-two would be hard, if not impossible. I had no bills, so if I had to scrub floors, I would do fine. I also started getting my social security and put every penny of it in my retirement fund. My funds were growing faster now. I kidded Darchele that I would probably be a bag lady when I got older and would need her help. I was worried that it might be true.

My mom and I got rid of most the stuff in the house. We had a lot because we had double stuff when we moved in together. The house was about empty when done. We decided to take essentials and buy all new furniture when we got there. We kept two bedroom sets and got rid of two. We got rid of most of the living room furniture, and only kept what kitchen things we thought we would need for the two of us.

The house went up for sale and unbelievably sold in less than a week to the first person who looked at it. What a shock. That made me believe that I had made the right decision because I believed that whenever things are right, we are provided with the means and the opportunity to fulfill the task. Everyone at work could hardly believe it. They put their ad out and after a couple weeks found someone for me to train in inventory and purchasing.

Since I was already working my overtime remotely from home, I agreed to continue monitoring the Crystal reports for them from Missouri since they had no one else in the company who could do it.

Darchele had an apartment set up for us where she and Tony were living at that time, and we moved in. We wanted time to look for a place to buy and didn't want to hurry. We thought a year in the apartment would give us time to get to know the area.

Shortly after we moved to Missouri, Darchele and Tony bought a house. It was about fifteen miles from the apartment. I knew we would buy near her, so I started looking for a job in that area. I went on several good interviews, but I was taking my time. About three months went by, and I finally found one that I thought would be a good fit. I was not putting my age on any of my applications, and fortunately, I looked younger than I was, and no one said anything about it. The person who interviewed me told me they called Evan for a reference, and he gave me a great one.

That call must have scared Evan because he was on the phone with me that day and said the girl they hired was not working out. Since everything I did was on the computer, would I consider working remotely full time from Missouri? I was thrilled; of course, I would. Now I didn't have to learn a new job. I was offered the job in Missouri the next day. I told them what happened, and they said they would keep my application and if it didn't work out to let him know. We found a beautiful new villa about six miles away from Darchele and Tony. We filled it with new furniture and were as happy as could be.

I have now worked seventeen years from home. It was the greatest thing that ever happened to me. I would go in and work from the office in Michigan for a week, once a year, until about eight years ago. Other than that, I was able to care for my mother at home in her later years, until she passed peacefully at home on October 6, 2014, at the ripe old age of ninety-three.

I am comfortable now, thanks to my mother who left the villa in a trust for me, to stay in as long as I lived or until I gave it up. Then it would be sold and divided between us five kids. With my social security and the interest from my investments, I have everything I need. I am satisfied.

I will be seventy-nine December 2021, and am still working as a consultant for Mason's. I am on call and put in a few hours a week helping them through problems and supporting Crystal Reports. Smartphones have been a great invention. With them, I can be anywhere when they need me. It freed me up to run errands, or go shopping, and still be available. I get emails on my phone, so if they wanted me to see something, they could email the document, and I could open it on my phone if I weren't home—what a great deal.

I have been working for Mason's thirty-three years now. I no longer live in fear of losing my job and can deal with people without fear.

Life is good. I have found a happiness I never knew existed. While working at Mason's, my personal life went on in peace, and my work life improved one hundred percent.

When Darchele was nine, her father started dating a waitress named Linda and got her pregnant. What an idiot. They moved in together, and they had a little girl, Amy.

Darchele got to know her a little bit. This was a troubled little girl, and I felt bad for her. When she was about eight, Darrow was taken to court for molesting her, and Linda for failure to protect. The stories we heard about how she had been treated were awful.

The lawyer asked Darchele to testify in court about her father. She was seventeen at this time, and Linda had a daughter about Darchele's age, who was living with her father. They also asked Linda's daughter to come to court. Darrow pleaded "no contest," and the girls didn't need to go in and tell their experiences with him, which was good. Amy was put in foster care. Darrow and Linda split up not long after that.

Darchele got a call and was told that on March 10, 2007, her dad had crashed his car into a tree. He was in the ICU and not expected to live. As his next of kin, they needed her to come. She called me, and I went with her. We stayed with him until he passed on March 21, 2007.

They had him on life support, and she had to decide if it should be removed, and it was hard for her. She said she felt like she was treating him like a dog. I told her to call his brother and sister and ask them what they thought, and everyone agreed it was best to do it. She had him removed from life support, and he passed within an hour. We both cried. I still loved the man I had married.

We learned a lot about his years there in Terre Haute, Indiana, while taking care of his affairs. He had been going by the name Frank M. Von Ray, and they referred to him as "Crazy Frank," but everyone liked him. We had a memorial for him there and were surprised at how many people showed up. Darchele's half-sister, Amy, even came; she was twenty-one then, and Darchele was thirty-two.

Darrow's sister brought a display of pictures, and Darchele brought the uniform that he had in his apartment. His sister brought an 8 x 10 picture of him in his uniform. He was a good-looking man and officer. Everyone was so surprised that he had once been an officer in the Navy and lived quite a normal life for many years. They had only seen "Crazy Frank."

We were pleased to share some of his former life with everyone, and happy to see he had so many friends, and a peaceful life there, even if it was a bit "crazy."

In the Light

1993-2019

Dear God,
 Thank you, thank you, and thank you. I will never forget to listen for your "still small voice" for guidance.
 Isaiah 65:24, "...before they call, I will answer; and while they are yet speaking, I will hear.
  Much Love,
  Michele

Both my home life and work life are peaceful now. I am the same person at home and at work. The two conflicting sides of me are no longer in conflict. What more could I want?

The Bible states in Genesis, "And God said, Let us make man in our image, after our likeness:" This likeness must be spiritual, since God is Spirit, and like produces like.

Another eye-opener in that quote is the word "our." To me, that meant there are two aspects to God; he is both Comforter and Protector. Those are male and female qualities, so God is not just Father;

he is both Father and Mother. To me, that means if we are his complete image, that we *all* have both those qualities. As God's reflection, my actions would express all his qualities.

Our Constitution and Bill of Rights, declares, "Man is endowed by his Maker with certain inalienable rights, among which are life, liberty, and the pursuit of happiness." I knew I was on my way.

Darchele taught me about computers, which made me more valuable in my job. My church gave me the tools I needed to live in this world, peacefully on the job, and in my personal life. Serving on the board at church gave me experience on how to chair meetings and talk in front of a group of people, which was a big help when I had to conduct meetings at work.

My religion, Christian Science, and the textbook, *Science and Health with Key to the Scriptures* by Mary Baker Eddy, along with the Bible, taught me to trust God, Mind, Principle, and to reason through things logically. That helped me through the many challenges that came up in my life. I was mesmerized by my past and could not break through it until I found Christian Science. Science is normally thought of as the demonstrable laws of the physical universe. Christian Science is the demonstrable laws of the Spiritual universe, as applied to the human condition, and as taught by Christ Jesus. I love Christian Science, it works, and it has completely changed the course of my life.

When I started going to church, I heard the word *logic* a lot, so I enrolled in the local junior college and took a course in logic. I needed to know what it was and how it related to my life. When I picked up the textbook and looked in the back, I was ready to give up. It looked like a foreign language. My boss told me to stop looking at the end of the book and start from the front. Well, I couldn't believe I aced the class. I guess I wasn't so stupid after all. It opened my eyes to the many misconceptions I had.

Life was looking up. I still have much to learn, but I have reached the point where I'm happy. Always remember, "Revenge is inadmissible." It keeps you in the darkness. You can never get even.

When I look back, I know that God was always there protecting me. I don't think I would be here today if both my work life and my personal life were a mess at the same time. I needed some peace in my life somewhere to survive it.

Mary Baker Eddy writes in *Science and Health*, Page 57:15-30: "Beauty, wealth, or fame is incompetent to meet the demands of the affections, and should never weigh against the better claims of intellect, goodness, and virtue. Happiness is spiritual, born of Truth and Love. It is unselfish; therefore, it cannot exist alone but requires all mankind to share it.

"Human affection is not poured forth vainly, even though it meets no return. Love enriches the nature, enlarging, purifying, and elevating it. The wintry blasts of earth may uproot the flowers of affection, and scatter them to the winds; but this severance of fleshly ties serves to unite thought more closely to God, for Love supports the struggling heart until it ceases to sigh over the world and begins to unfold its wings for heaven."

I finally know that I'm neither unattractive nor stupid. For many years, I believed that lie, but now I understand that as God's reflection, I have all his qualities, including beauty and intelligence. Beauty radiates from within.

Darchele and I talked about when she was growing up, because I had concerns that her life was not as good as it should have been. She told me she had a good life and had no complaints. Maybe I shouldn't have worried so much, but I did. I don't think she remembers some of the bad times, or she didn't see them the way I did. I believe God protected her from my trauma.

When I think back now, even though I didn't have much money or time to take her to special events, our friends at church took her to many places. She saw *Phantom of the Opera, Cats,* and the Ice Capades, and was even taken skiing. That is more than many kids get to do.

Darchele and Tony have given me no grandchildren, but that is okay. I do have two granddogs, Thor and Zeus. They are happy, and that is all that counts. They both have good jobs and travel the world on their vacations. I couldn't be happier for them.

I have two beautiful cats, littermates, Sugar and Spice, which give me all the affection and joy I could ever want. It is a pleasure living with them.

I read a lot, which I could never do while I was working. I go to church twice a week. I'm not implying I am a "Miss Goody Two Shoes." Believe me I make my share of mistakes, but I'm trying, and that's what makes my life so interesting now. I take care of the church finances and do the payroll. I still work a few hours for Mason's. I go out to dinner and the movies with my neighbor occasionally. We even watch TV together at her place or mine. She is my best friend and a place where I can talk about anything and not be judged. I think she feels the same.

I go out to lunch every day to get out of the house. I have been eating at the same place, Burkempers, for fifteen years now. The server, Crystal, has worked there for about thirty-three years. She is always happy and easy to chat with. She remembers everyone's orders, and the service is excellent. She told me about this place called Curves where she exercises, and now I meet her there every weekday afternoon when she gets off work. Cathy, the trainer, always chats with everyone and keeps up on their lives. It is a friendly, fun place to exercise.

I eat healthy foods. I feel good, both mentally and physically. My weight is down, and all is well with the world. I have been single for over forty years now and do not miss having a man in my life, not that there is anything wrong with men. There are many good men out there.

The most important things I have learned over the years are to love myself, and that one can't love until they forgive. To forgive is not for the other person, it is for you. It means to give up all your anger, your fear, your frustrations, your hatred, your resentment, and your desire for revenge. When you do this, you are free to Love, to find peace and harmony in your life.

Over the years, the hate I thought I felt toward others who were mistreating me was really self-hate. Now I understand that we are all God's children, are unique and special, and have a place on this earth that no one else can fill. We are a loving expression of our creator. When we learn to love ourselves, our inner light will shine outward and bless all those around us.

Don't get me wrong; I'm not a finished product. There are times when I'm afraid to open my mouth for fear that something stupid will come flying out of it. Then I remember what Moses said to God about him not being eloquent of speech, and God told him he would put the words in his mouth. Then I relax and know that God won't let me say something stupid, not if I listen for his guidance.

Exodus 4:10-12, "And Moses said unto the LORD, O my Lord, I *am* not eloquent, neither heretofore, nor since thou hast spoken unto thy servant: but I *am* slow of speech, and of a slow tongue. And the LORD said unto him, Who hath made man's mouth? ...Now therefore go, and I will be with thy mouth, and teach thee what thou shalt say."

I have found the Bible is a great self-help book. If you can get past all the "thee" and "thou" the "begets" and "begats," and find the messages, it comes to life for you. My favorite books are Genesis Chapter 1 through the third verse in Chapter 2, the Psalms, and all the New Testament, especially the four Gospels. Jesus mapped out the way for us. He showed how our relationship with God worked. He said in John 5:30, "I can of mine own self do nothing: as I hear, I judge: and my judgment is just; because I seek not mine own will, but the will of the Father which hath sent me."

"I can of mine own self do nothing." When I try to do things myself, things don't seem to work out the way I intended. However, if I listen for that "still small voice," God's directions, and do it his way, everything turns out better. It is a hard lesson to learn, but he is there for us 24/7. I needed to learn to listen and to hear. If you do this, you will never regret it.

Take care of your thoughts; they are your most precious assets. From Romans 12:2 "Be not conformed to this world: but be ye transformed by the renewing of your mind, that ye may prove what is that good, and acceptable, and perfect, will of God."

My way may not be your way, but if you are suffering from the results of abuse, I strongly recommend that you find something to take your mind off ruminating over the past. Focus your thought upward and outward, on something that gives you joy and pleasure that makes you feel better and helps you forget the misery of your past. Changing the way you think does not happen overnight, but there is no time like the present to start. Make the best of your present, and the future will take care of itself.

"Brethren, I count not myself to have apprehended: but this one thing I do, forgetting those things which are behind, and reaching forth unto those things which are before, I press toward the mark for the prize of the high calling of God in Christ Jesus." (Philippians 3:13, 14).

I have found my purpose in life. It is to Love all mankind and to glorify God.

Matthew 22:36-39, "Master, which *is* the great commandment in the law? Jesus said unto him, Thou shalt love the Lord thy God with all thy heart, and with all thy soul, and with all thy mind. This is the first and great commandment. And the second *is* like unto it, Thou shalt love thy neighbour as thyself."

To love your neighbor "as thyself" means you must love yourself first. As they say on the airlines, when the oxygen mask drops, put yours on first, so you can help others.

This is my story. If I have reached one person and given you a little hope that life can be better, then I have accomplished my goal. Luke 12:32 "Fear not, little flock; for it is your Father's good pleasure to give you the kingdom."

My love goes out to all the struggling hearts. I made it through the darkness and into the light, and so can you.

Acknowledgements

This is probably the only book I will ever write, but I enjoy writing and blog regularly on my website. I also do a podcast on Prayerful Living internet radio every Friday.

Telling my story has released me from my past. I started over thirty years ago, and then it sat in a box until a friend, who knew much of my life, said, "You should write a book." Since I'm retired now and had the time, I dug it out and sorted through the papers and started to put it together. My journals provided me with many facts that could have been forgotten over the years.

Many people in my book are gone now, but my siblings are still present and approve of me telling my story. My daughter also supports my efforts. She lives elsewhere with her husband, so she didn't have to put up with me while I did this.

With encouragement from a friend, Irene Rock, I started. She read each chapter as I wrote it and let me know when she didn't think I had gone far enough explaining something or had gone too far. All her encouragement kept me going.

I joined a group called Saturday Writers, and after every meeting, I'd come home and edit my book with the new things I learned about writing. Even after many edits, it wasn't ready to publish. Jeanne

Felfe, an editor whom I met at Saturday Writers and the author of *Bridge to Us*, agreed to edit my book.

I am so grateful to her as all her recommendations made it read much better. Jeanne also recommended I change the title. It had been "A Chronicle of Choices, From Abuse to Absolution." That was a bit wordy. I'd used the phrase "out of the darkness and into the light" in the preface and on the last page of the book. Jeanne thought that would make a good title, and I agreed. So, it is now, *Out of Darkness, Into the Light: With Letters from Michele*.

While working on the book, my two sweet kitties, Sugar and Spice, didn't always get fed on time, but they were patient and would rub around my legs until I reached a stopping point.

If you know someone who could benefit from my story, please recommend my book.

I wasn't educated to be an author, but with a lot of help, this is happening.

I hope you gleaned something from my story. God bless you all.

Sincerely,

Michele

About the Author

To stay in touch with Michele:
Website: Lettersfrommichele.com
FB: Facebook.com/lettersfrommichele
PLIR:
https://prayerfulliving.com/healingmusic/inspiration-weekly.html

Michele's life was quite melodramatic until she was in her forties. She moved forty-nine times during her life, covering states from coast to coast.

She graduated from high school, and over the years, she educated herself and took college courses as needed for her jobs. She loves learning new things every day.

She has worked since she was sixteen and had a banking career for seventeen years. Then, she went into business doing Purchasing and Inventory

Management for the next forty-six years. She has worked from home for the last seventeen years and now works as a consultant.

Michele writes an inspirational blog bi-monthly about her experiences. And she does a podcast on Inspiration Weekly that airs Fridays on the Healing Music station of (PLIR) Prayerful Living Internet Radio. She has taught Sunday School and currently writes a monthly newsletter for her church. She was church treasurer for twelve years, has served on the board, and performed other functions for her church.

She lives alone with her two cats, Sugar and Spice. Michele is happy, exercises, eats right, reads a lot, and has a good life. She lives six miles from her married daughter.

Made in the USA
Monee, IL
10 January 2022